31 Daily Devotions with Annual Reflection and Journaling Pages

Reflecting on Christmas Past

Heather Greer

©2023 Heather Greer

Published by Scrivenings Press LLC
15 Lucky Lane
Morrilton, Arkansas 72110
https://ScriveningsPress.com

Printed in the United States of America

All rights reserved. No part of this publication may be reproduced, stored in a retrieval system, or transmitted in any form or by any means—for example, electronic, photocopy and recording— without the prior written permission of the publisher. The only exception is brief quotation in printed reviews.

Paperback ISBN 978-1-64917-341-6

eBook ISBN 978-1-64917-342-3

Editor: Mike Ehret

Cover by Linda Fulkerson
www.bookmarketinggraphics.com

Scripture are taken from the NEW AMERICAN STANDARD BIBLE(r), Copyright (c) 1960,1962,1963,1968,1971,1972,1973,1975,1977 by The Lockman Foundation. Used by permission. www.lockman.org.

NO AI TRAINING: Without in any way limiting the author's [and publisher's] exclusive rights under copyright, any use of this publication to "train" generative artificial intelligence (AI) technologies to generate text is expressly prohibited. The author reserves all rights to license uses of this work for generative AI training and development of machine learning language models.

To everyone seeking God's peace, love, and joy this Christmas. I pray you find them as you draw closer to Him.

Contents

Dear Reader …	1
A Time to Remember	3
A Time for Remembering	5
The Reason—Day One	11
The Reason—Day Two	13
The Reason—Day Three	15
The Reason—Day Four	17
The Reason—Day Five	21
Reflecting on the Reason	23
The Setting—Day One	29
The Setting—Day Two	31
The Setting—Day Three	33
The Setting—Day Four	37
The Setting—Day Five	39
Reflecting on the Setting	41
The People—Day One	47
The People—Day Two	51
The People—Day Three	55
The People—Day Four	59
The People—Day Five	63
Reflecting on the People	67
The Sounds—Day One	73
The Sounds—Day Two	75
The Sounds—Day Three	79
The Sounds—Day Four	81
The Sounds—Day Five	83
Reflecting on the Sounds	87
The Gift—Day One	93
The Gift—Day Two	97
The Gift—Day Three	99
The Gift—Day Four	101
The Gift—Day Five	103
Reflecting on the Gifts	107

The Love—Day One	113
The Love—Day Two	115
The Love—Day Three	117
The Love—Day Four	119
The Love—Day Five	121
Reflecting on the Love	123
Your Christmas Heritage	127
Annual Reflection Pages	129
Hosting a Reflecting on Christmas Past Event	147
About the Author	151
Also by Heather Greer	153

Dear Reader...

Why reflect on Christmas Past?

The weeks from Thanksgiving to New Year's Day often pass in a blur. We feel pressed to deliver a picture-perfect Christmas and that takes a toll on our emotional, physical, and spiritual health. Amid all the activity, it's easy to set aside one of the most spiritually significant times of year to focus on our deep to-do lists.

Reflecting on Christmas Past is designed for annual use. Though it can be useful any time during the Christmas season, I recommend starting on November 24th. This timeline will encourage putting meaning into your holiday.

After the introductory devotion, readings are divided into six themes, containing five devotions each. Each section of five devotions ends with journaling space for you to reflect on the message and record your memories. Your reflections will help move truth from your head to your heart and spur you into action.

This unique devotional also serves as a journal to record future holidays. The Your Christmas Heritage and Annual Reflection pages give additional space to consider the devotional themes. When full, the journal is a collection of memories from your Christmases past.

May God speak to your heart through each devotion, giving this Christmas and those to come renewed focus on Him.

Heather Greer

A Time to Remember

Luke 2:19 "But Mary treasured all these things, pondering them in her heart."

Luke 2:51 "And He went down with them and came to Nazareth, and He continued in subjection to them; and His mother treasured all these things in her heart."

Mary pondered. Probably more than most new mothers, she considered deeply the events surrounding her child's birth. She held those happenings safely tucked away in her heart. God's Word, the Bible, tells us this, but why? The gospels lay out all the details surrounding the birth of Jesus. Why did God deem Mary's ponderings important enough to let us in on her mindset as she considered each detail of her Son's birth?

Mary remembered. She is in good company! Looking through Scripture, especially in the Old Testament, we see remembering is important to God.

When the Israelites experienced God's provision in separating the waters of the Jordan River in Joshua 4, God commanded them to set up 12 stones after the crossing in a place of remembrance. When God established the celebration of Purim, it was to remember God's salvation of Israel from Haman.

Every part of the Passover seder is God reminding His people of their time as slaves in Egypt, His intervention to free them, and His promises for their future. But remembrance also takes a front row seat in the New Testament at Jesus's final celebration of the Passover meal. At that time, He tied past events into what He was about to accomplish for mankind and told His disciples to "do this in remembrance of me."

Why does God want us to remember? Does He want His followers stuck in the glory days? Absolutely not. God encourages us to recall these times, so the lessons learned about who God is, how He works, and who they are to Him will not be lost. He did it to give us a spiritual heritage to pass down from generation to generation that will strengthen our faith, give us peace, and provide us with true hope in the midst of our struggles.

Mary pondered God's fulfillment of prophecy in the birth of Jesus. She remembered the shepherds' worship, the angels' message, and the wise men's gifts. Later, as her son grew, she would hold onto the memory of His passion to be about His father's purpose.

As a mother, I firmly believe those memories came to mind 33 years later as she watched her innocent son, her firstborn child, hanging on a cross. She knew this was part of God's plan. But I believe as she helplessly watched her son's anguish and death, Mary's heart broke and all of the things she'd pondered and tucked away came flooding to her mind to give her a measure of strength and hope.

This is what comes from remembering the past workings of God in our lives. We see it in the rituals of the various Old Testament feasts. We see it in the practice of communion as Jesus instructed it to be done. And if we look through the events of our lives, we will see it there too.

Daily Reflection: This Christmas season take time to remember both your physical and spiritual heritage. As you ponder these memories, open your heart to the messages God has for you and reflect on how He has worked in your past.

A Time for Remembering

Mary pondered. Now it's your turn. Think about a time when God has worked in your life. It could be a time when God spoke to you, worked through you, or worked through someone else for your benefit. It may not include shepherds and angels on a hillside, but that doesn't mean it isn't an important piece of your spiritual heritage. A memory you turn to for peace, strength, and hope.

My spiritual heritage:

_____
_____
_____
_____
_____
_____
_____
_____

Now focus on Christmas specifically. Try to recall one special Christmas that has stayed with you through the years. It may be spiritually related, but it doesn't have to be.

My Christmas Heritage:

_____
_____
_____
_____
_____
_____
_____

Why is this particular Christmas memory so meaningful to you?

_____
_____
_____
_____
_____
_____
_____

Looking at your thoughts about this Christmas, can you pinpoint in a few words what made this time special? Was it family time, a time of giving, or possibly a heartfelt gift? Sum up what's special in three to four words.

_____

As you go into this Christmas season, let this special memory of the past point you toward what makes a holiday season special. Give attention this year to including activities related to that theme. You're not trying to recreate Christmas past, but rather focusing your time on the things you find most memorable and meaningful in the holiday.

Be careful not to make this one more thing on your to-do list. With Christmas often comes a demanding schedule. Our goal is not to cram more in. It is to help you know which things to cut and which things to embrace. Taking time to learn what means the most to you is a great way to start that process.

The Reason

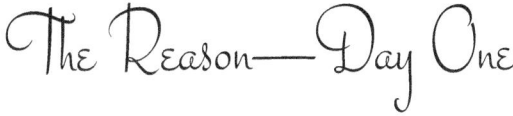

Genesis 3:14-15 "The LORD God said to the serpent, Because you have done this, Cursed are you more than all the cattle, And more than every beast of the field; On your belly you will go, And dust you will eat all the days of your life; And I will put enmity between you and the woman, and between your seed and her seed; He shall bruise you on the head, And you shall bruise him on the heel."

It's easy to run ourselves ragged trying to make the holiday resemble a Norman Rockwell painting. Is every present wrapped with a beautiful bow? Can we rearrange schedules to attend each party we're invited to? If we make a trip to the store on the other side of town, will the perfect gift for Mr. Hard-to-Buy-For be waiting for us near the check-out counter?

In the flurry of activity, it's easy to forget there is a reason for the time we're celebrating. We give lip service to Jesus being the reason for the season, but do we take time to reflect on what that means?

The Old Testament is full of prophecies about the coming Savior. While Isaiah contains what are probably the most quoted Christmas prophecies, it's far from the first book to include them. As early as the third chapter of Genesis, we see references to the promise of the Savior as well as the reason why we needed Him in the first place.

Three chapters into the history of the world and people had already sinned against God. With one bite of forbidden fruit the relationship was destroyed. We could never be good enough to undo the damage, and our holy God cannot allow sin in His presence.

The problem required a divine solution. God loves His creation, including us. The idea of eternity without those He created in His image, those He breathed life into, was not acceptable. Even as He disciplined the parties involved and set out their curses, God gave hint to the promise of future reconciliation.

While people messed up at every turn, God patiently and lovingly provided a temporary answer in the form of the Old Testament's sacrificial system. It wasn't given to secure our salvation but to show how we needed to rely fully on God's provision to cleanse us of sin once and for all. Ritual sacrifice created a picture of God's plan of salvation that we could grasp so when the Savior finally came, we could better understand why His sacrifice was needed.

Focusing on the reason we celebrate at Christmas doesn't mean we have to give up our activities and traditions. But through reflecting on the reason for our celebration, we gain the necessary perspective to put each activity in its rightful place. It can even add spiritual depth to our traditions.

Daily Reflection: As Christians, we're quick to say, "Jesus is the reason for the season." And that's true. But there is a reason we needed Jesus in the first place.

Looking at previous celebrations of His birth, can you recall any event, song, or reading that impressed on you the reason why we need Jesus's birth? What could help you move your focus from celebrating Jesus's birth to celebrating His birth as the starting point for our forgiveness of sin? What could help you remember our salvation is the real reason for the season?

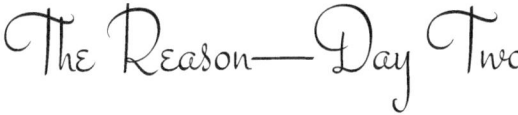

Isaiah 9:6-7 "For a child will be born to us, a son will be given to us; and the government will rest on His shoulders; And His name will be called Wonderful Counselor, Mighty God, Eternal Father, Prince of Peace. There will be no end to the increase of His government or of peace, On the throne of David and over his kingdom, To establish it and to uphold it with justice and righteousness From then on and forevermore. The zeal of the LORD of hosts will accomplish this."

Do you remember your Christmas presents from last year? The year before? How about from Christmas eight years ago?

The more years in the past, the less I remember. And I'm not talking about generic gifts from an office party. I mean gifts someone took great care in choosing for me. If I walk through my house, I'll recognize some of them. But intentionally trying to remember brings less than satisfactory results, especially the further back I reach.

A few gifts are forever imprinted in my memories. There is one reason I remember these. They are gifts I regularly use.

I use a mug my son and daughter-in-law gave me several times a week. My husband and I record our special days in a journal my daughter gave us for that purpose. The pair of high-top Crayola Converse shoes another son gifted me because he knows of my love for both crayons and Converse are worn any time my outfit allows it. The DVDs from my youngest let my husband and I return to a favorite show time and again.

This wide variety of gifts given by my loved ones are tied together by one thread: I use them. With their use comes my ability to recall the giver and the occasion. In fact, every use brings fresh appreciation for the gift and the one who gave it.

In sending Jesus, God gave us a universally needed gift. He provided the way to be forgiven for our sins and restored in relationship with Him. But God gave us so much more when He gave us Jesus. We also received the Wonderful Counselor, the Mighty God, the Eternal Father, the Prince of Peace.

Even on days when my need of a Savior isn't staring me in the face, I need the rest of who Jesus is. I need His peace when life becomes a stormy sea. Jesus's counsel is far above worldly counsel in helping me make wise decisions. I need a Father who knows me and knows what is best for me. And when the enemy pursues me, I need the mightiest God.

When we meditate on all Jesus is to us, the gift that He is becomes more precious. When we see who He really is, we appreciate more what He chose to give up. As Christmas nears each year, we celebrate not just His birth, but also the gift Jesus is every day of the year.

Daily Reflection: When do you see Jesus as more than the baby in the manger or the Savior on the cross? Are there times in your Christmas celebrations that remind you He is the Wonderful Counselor, Mighty God, Everlasting Father, and Prince of Peace?

As you go through this Christmas season, be alert for the times when Jesus shows who He is in your days. Thank Him for being your peace, your strength, your patience—whatever else you need. If you find yourself needing a specific gift He brings, what can you do to help foster that characteristic?

The Reason—Day Three

Ephesians 2:8-9 "For by grace you have been saved through faith; and that not of yourselves, it is the gift of God; not as a result of works, so that no one may boast."

Christmas was going to be sparse at our house that year.

When my husband's position was eliminated, his only option was taking another job at an extreme pay cut. This left us with bills acquired when the salary made them more manageable, four children to feed, and no way to supplement his income in time for the holiday. Bills would all be paid, but it left little to no extra. We didn't talk about it with others, but we definitely felt the weight of the deficit.

Only our Christmas traditions would suffer. Nothing could keep us from celebrating Jesus. But Christmas baking, gift giving, and even new clothes for Christmas services would take a hit. And there was nothing we could do.

God stepped into our holiday through a couple we've been close friends with for years. We'd said nothing to them about our limitations. But this couple felt God calling them to bless a family, and they felt that family should be ours. Imagine my surprise, joy, and humble gratitude when I opened their Christmas card and found God had used them to ease our situation that Christmas.

It wasn't the first time God moved on our behalf at Christmas. He's been doing it for centuries. After all, providing for us what we cannot provide for ourselves is what Christmas is all about.

Jesus didn't leave the splendor of heaven with its eternal worship, glory, and power to become "God with us" so we could have a fun family holiday. He didn't come to bring tidings of great joy to fuel our songs for years to come. Peace, love, and a spirit of giving are all wonderful, but when we take them at face value, we miss the real reason we need Christmas. The reason that illuminates the true meaning behind the joy, peace, love, and spirit of giving.

The reason Jesus allowed Himself to be humbled to a manger first and then a cross was because there was a need only He could fill.

Our sin was so great, there was no hope of reconciliation. There was no way to know peace with our Heavenly Father. We couldn't give enough to pay our own bill because every sinful action and attitude added daily to mounting debt. Short of offering ourselves up for an eternity of torment separated from God, we were and still are powerless to erase the debt of our sin.

But God. His love for us, His desire to be known by us, moved Him to intercede when we could not. Though we were the ones who spiritually spent more than we could ever repay, God stepped in to restore us. To pay our debt we could never pay on our own. That is the reason for the season.

Daily Reflection: Often, we give nativity scenes places of honor in our homes at Christmas, but how often do we fail to consider who the baby in the manger is, what He gave up, or why He gave it up? What decorations, music, readings, or traditions have reminded you about the true reason for Christmas? Celebration of Jesus's birth is richer when we allow the reason for it to sink deep into our hearts. What will help you focus on God's gift of salvation this Christmas?

The Reason—Day Four

Galatians 4:4-5 "But when the fullness of the time came, God sent forth His Son, born of a woman, born under the Law, so that He might redeem those who were under the Law, that we might receive the adoption as sons."

Growing up, Christmas dinner meant the whole family gathered together around my grandma's table sharing a meal, laughter, and telling stories. We left with bellies full—our hearts, too.

But our family wasn't only family. My grandmother had two children. My uncle had two children, and my mother had three. Including my great-grandma, my grandparents and the spouses, a total of twelve people should have filled our table each year.

However, in all my Christmas memories, I cannot recall a time when only a dozen people shared the meal. More often than not, there were seventeen. As grandkids aged, the numbers jumped closer to twenty-five. Yet, even with the additions, it was still family at the table.

I had only one blood uncle, but God blessed me with additional aunts, uncles, and cousins. These honorary relatives were close family friends. Their kids grew up with us. We worshiped together. We shared Sunday and holiday meals because family isn't just about sharing blood.

Family is all the people you choose to share life with. My grandparents set that example. I've carried it into our home. My children's best friends call me mom. They love their mothers. We just offer another place to belong. Especially at Christmas, my door is always open to them as family. Because family is what I choose for them to be.

Others have honorary aunts and uncles. My grandparents didn't start the idea of family by choice. God did. And we see it clearly at Christmas.

God used the birth of His Son to offer each of us a place to belong. We're no longer spiritual orphans. We aren't on our own against the world, relying only on ourselves to make it through life.

Sin loses its claim on our souls when we accept that Jesus came as a baby, lived as one of His creations, and died on the cross as an innocent. But God didn't stop with merely offering us salvation, though it would've been within His rights to do so.

God could have saved us to be puppets unable to do or think. At our moment of salvation, God could have transformed us into angels praising at His throne.

He didn't. He wants our lives to honor Him. God could have left us as servants, but He offered friendship instead. When He might have stopped at friendship, God went further, making us family.

Scripture tells us God has adopted us as His sons and daughters. This comes with all the rights and privileges of family because through Jesus's blood we are family. Everyone who has accepted God's gift of salvation is in God's family.

Because the first Christmas led to the first Easter, we have family greater than we could ever imagine. We've been adopted for eternity into God's family. And that means, we can spend each Christmas celebrating at God's table.

Daily Reflection: Who fills the seats at your Christmas table? Consider your past Christmases. How have you experienced the blessing of being part of God's family? What turns your heart to the truth that because of

Christmas, you have been adopted into God's family? How might you share that truth with others and experience the joy of expanded family this Christmas?

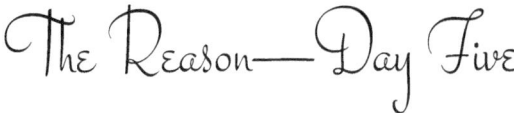

Matthew 1:21 "She will bear a Son; and you shall call His name Jesus, for He will save His people from their sins."

December babies have it rough, especially those whose birthdays fall close to one of the most celebrated holidays of the year. I was blessed to have my birthday fall early in the month. My special day was far enough away from Christmas to prevent the dreaded Christmas/birthday combo.

Some of my friends, though, were not so lucky. With birthdays falling immediately before or after, their families held Christmas themed birthday parties to save on decorations. Sometimes, due to outside holiday obligations, the families were too busy with Christmas events to even host parties.

These unfortunate children often fared no better in the gifting arena, with one gift sometimes covering both Christmas and their birthday. Yes, the point of Christmas is not the gifts. But no child enjoys having their special day hijacked by another holiday. All their friends get birthday *and* Christmas presents. And their friends not born in December, never received birthday presents wrapped in Christmas trees, snowflakes, or angels.

But the unfortunate union may not stop with combining the celebrations. Sometimes those born closest to the twenty-fifth end up carrying reminders of that coincidence with them the rest of their lives through the names they were given: Joy Noelle, Christmas Holly, Gloria, Gabriel, Carol, Noel, Ivy and Merri top the list of oft-chosen Christmas names given to children sharing their birthdays with Jesus.

However, the name given to Mary's baby on that first Christmas wasn't attached to seasonal decorations or festive activities. But it is a name that carries the idea of Christmas each time it is called on. "You shall call His name Jesus." Why? Because "Jesus" means "Yahweh saves." Each time we say our Lord's name, we're asking God to save His people from their sins. Jesus literally means "God is salvation."

Not God *provides* salvation. Not God *will bring* salvation. The name is so much bigger than that. God is salvation. That tiny baby placed in the manger the first Christmas isn't simply how God provides salvation. *He is the salvation.*

Jesus is God. God made man. God with us. Emmanuel. And that's a reason to celebrate!

Daily Reflection: Consider songs you've heard that draw your attention to the meaning behind the names Jesus and Emmanuel. Do they cause you to pause what you're doing and reflect on the real reason for Christmas? Consider creating a special Christmas playlist that focuses on Jesus as our salvation and God with us. Allow those songs to usher in a time of personal reflection on the reason for our celebration. If you have trouble finding songs, here are some to start your ponderings. "O Come, O Come Emmanuel", "Emmanuel (Hallowed Manger Ground)", "He Shall Reign Forevermore", and "This is Christmas."

Reflecting on the Reason

From Thanksgiving to Christmas day, we cram our schedules full. Today, as you journal your reflections, think about why we need Christmas and what it means to us that God sent Jesus as our Savior. It's easy to look at the big picture need of the world, but don't stop there. Approach your reflection from the perspective of a personalized John 3:16: "For God so loved (insert your name), that He gave His only begotten Son, that when (insert your name) believes in Him, (she/he) shall not perish, but have eternal life."

Begin with prayer. Ask God to open your heart to truths that may not be easy to consider. When you have finished your prayer, read the following verses. Take care not to dismiss the familiar, but to dig deeper.

Romans 3:23, Galatians 5:19-21, Isaiah 64:6, Mark 7:20-23, 1 John 2:15, James 3:16

Are you struggling with any of the sins listed in the Scriptures above? Or is it another sin you've been holding onto that keeps you from enjoying close fellowship with God? Be honest with yourself and God. Bring them to Him in the space below and let Him show you your need for the Savior this Christmas.

_____
_____
_____
_____
_____
_____
_____

Now read the following verses that show what Christmas does for you:

Hebrews 9:14, Psalm 32:1, Titus 2:14, Romans 6:23, 2 Corinthians 5:21, Ephesians 1:7

Use the space below to express what it means to you that God would be willing to sacrifice the Son He loved in order to take care of the sin that was wholly yours.

_____
_____
_____
_____
_____
_____
_____

Look back through the Christmas seasons in your past. Are there any that stand out as times when the real reason for celebration was impressed on you? What was it about that time that drew your focus toward your need and God's provision, and away from the sparkly extras of the season?

_____
_____
_____

REFLECTING ON CHRISTMAS PAST

_____
_____
_____
_____
_____

What are a few practical steps you can take to ensure the true meaning of Christmas doesn't get lost in the hustle and bustle this year? If this is difficult, look back at your previous answer. You can't recreate those experiences, but you can learn from and gain direction from them.

_____
_____
_____
_____
_____
_____
_____
_____

If you've never considered your need for a Savior, I pray the verses shared today speak to you. We all have sinful hearts, and sin separates us from God. We can never be good enough to fix that broken relationship, but the good news is we don't have to be. God has done it for us. It started with Jesus in the manger and led to Him hanging on a cross. When the tomb was empty three days later our way to forgiveness was complete. Forgiveness of our sins and a restored relationship with our Heavenly Father is His gift of love to us and the reason we celebrate.

If you believe this and desire God's forgiveness, all you have to do is ask. God is waiting to forgive and welcome you into His family. He has the perfect Christmas gift for you. You can use the prayer below as a guide if you aren't sure what you want to say.

Father, I know I have sinned against you. I know that Your holiness requires punishment for sin and that the punishment is death and eternal separation from You. But I also believe You love me, and You don't want to be apart from me. You sent Jesus, Your Son, to die in my place. Forgive my sins and let me enjoy a relationship with You. Thank you for your gift of a Savior. Amen.

The Setting

The Setting—Day One

Luke 2:1-3, 11-12 "Now in those days a decree went out from Caesar Augustus, that a census be taken of all the inhabited earth. This was the first census taken while Quirinius was governor of Syria. And everyone was on his way to register for the census, each to his own city ... for today in the city of David there has been born for you a Savior, who is Christ the Lord. This will be a sign for you: you will find a baby wrapped in cloths and lying in a manger."

One year, for Christmas, my employer took all of us to The Fabulous Fox theater in St. Louis, Missouri, to see *Wicked*. I'd never been to a theater, other than small, local ones. And none at all since my college days.

The Fox was better than I could have imagined. As we walked up to the venue, the lights brightened the evening sky, drawing in passers-by. Posters beckoned with promises of beautiful sets and enjoyable shows. Inside, Christmas trees, rich colors, and elegant decorations set the tone. This would be a memorable evening.

Once seated, I scanned the theater. More trees. Distinctive architecture. And a dragon. Yes, a dragon hovered at the top of the stage. Before the curtain even rose, I was completely drawn in. Piqued solely by the scenery, I sat ready for the show.

Hollywood spends a fortune on set design, location shoots, and CGI. Why? Would you watch their film if actors performed on a blank stage? Of course not, and neither would I.

Think about your favorite book. Did the author weave the setting into the tale or leave you feeling like the story could happen any time, in any place? The environment increases the impact a story has on its readers.

While the reason for Jesus's birth is the most important aspect of the Christmas story, we gain greater depth of understanding when we consider the setting of the event. God could have sent Jesus to a wealthy family or even a royal family. Jesus could have been born with every privilege that would immediately garner Him the credibility and respect He deserved. But God chose a different setting.

The time of Roman rule. The City of David. A manger.

No piece of the Christmas story happened by chance. Each element was chosen by God in the writing of His story. Whether allowing us a glimpse into the desires of the Jewish people of the time, giving us a geographical picture, or reminding us that Jesus's story is for everyone, when we look at the setting God created for the salvation story, we come away with a greater appreciation of God's plan.

Daily Reflection: Not even the unimportant details of the Christmas story were left to chance. God orchestrated each one with purpose. As we look further into the setting of Jesus's birth, I pray we come to greater understanding of the truths God wove into the coming of His Son. This season, set aside time to consider the various traditions and events in your holiday. Is there purpose to them or do they only make demands on your time?

The Setting—Day Two

Micah 5:2 "But as for you, Bethlehem Ephrathah, Too little to be among the clans of Judah, From you One will go forth for Me to be ruler in Israel. His goings forth are from long ago, From the days of eternity."

I only remember one thing about Granny, my maternal great-grandmother, and Christmas. It's not a gift she gave. I'm not even sure she gave gifts. We didn't have a tradition of making cookies or going caroling. Granny didn't chop down a fresh tree and have everyone over to decorate it. I can't remember her even putting up an artificial tree.

Without other trappings of Christmas to distract me, I remember her small, ceramic Christmas tree. It was one of those vintage ceramic trees with colorful plastic bulbs that lit with the flick of a switch. They were popular in the sixties and seventies, and have recently made a comeback. Back then, Granny's tree wasn't yet vintage, but they had fallen out of popularity by the time I remember seeing it.

Every Christmas, Granny brought out her tree, not more than a foot tall. She'd clear off the little round table next to the recliner she sat in daily to embroider. For the next few weeks, the green tree with its colorful lights found a home in that spot.

I loved that tree. It captured my attention then and has remained clear in my memory since. When I began seeing the same style in stores again, I couldn't help myself. I bought two tiny white ones to place in my kitchen windows.

It's not that I think they're incredibly special as decorations go. My trees and hers aren't bold centerpieces of the holiday. They're small. They could be easily overlooked and forgotten. But they aren't because they're a tie to my Granny from Christmases past.

At the time of Jesus's birth, Bethlehem was insignificant. Too small to be a tribe of Judah. Nothing set it apart in the minds or hearts of those living in Israel. Definitely not the birthplace of a king, much less *the* King.

Only God knew better. He chose the least auspicious town in the area to be the birthplace of His Son. God does that a lot. Mary. A stable. Shepherds. Over and over again, not just in the Christmas story, God chooses the insignificant to house great purpose. He uses the humble and helpless to show His glory.

This comforts me and reminds me that we don't have to be more than we are. There's no need to pretend we have it all together, at Christmas or during any other season. Our name in lights—worldly success—will not garner any more attention for us from our Father.

God values what the world does not. He brings the purpose, the success, and the meaning. God treasures the small things, whether it's a ceramic tree full of memories, an uninspiring town, a person who feels less than special—or you living His purpose for your life.

Daily Reflection: It's easy to overlook the little things or take them for granted. Consider your Christmases past. What are some insignificant things God used to touch your heart in those seasons? Have you forgotten about those things in recent years, or do you still incorporate them into your celebrations? Are there any you can bring back?

The Setting—Day Three

Luke 2:7 "And she gave birth to her firstborn son; and she wrapped Him in cloths, and laid Him in a manger, because there was no room for them in the inn."

December driving is hazardous. At least, it is in the Midwest where I've lived my entire life. And I know places further north are even more so. It's a bit of a given: with winter weather comes treacherous road conditions.

For me, the ice and snow aren't the issue. Not even the extra congestion caused by last-minute shoppers. No, for me the biggest danger is far tinier. It's the twinkles.

Twinkling holiday lights are my kryptonite. More than spectacular fireworks displays in July, there is something otherworldly about Christmas lights in December. As my gaze wanders to the displays, my vehicle often follows. Not a great time for cause and effect to come into play.

Colored lights draped over houses. Inflatable snowmen waving to children and bringing smiles to all. Lights set to music. Together, they create a show that, for me, holds an energy unmatched by any singular decoration. When each house on the street joins in the decorating? Ah, bliss! That's when "walking in a winter wonderland" becomes real.

Out of all the Christmas decoration tableaus, my favorite is a window trimmed in lights that frames a beautifully decorated tree. I feel that family's invitation. And if simple white lights adorn the bushes and follow the rise and fall of the rooftop, I see twinkling Christmas stars fallen to earth for our enjoyment.

Simple but beautiful. But then, so is the real setting of the season.

God didn't choose a palace, even though Jesus deserved the biggest and the best. The walls of Jesus's birthplace weren't draped in ornate fabrics in vibrant colors befitting a King of the day. There wasn't even anyone to "leave the light on" for Jesus that night.

No. Jesus got a stable. And though most nativity sets show a modest lean-to constructed of wood, it's likely the barn was more cave than stable. Rough rock provided shelter from wind and rain but also blocked out the sunlight and moonbeams. And the holy family, rather than being the centerpiece of the display, was more likely shoehorned in wherever room allowed. And with livestock and less air flow? Let's just say Jesus didn't come into this world in a sweetly perfumed paradise.

John 3:16 tells us Jesus came to save the world. His birthplace emphasizes this point. If Jesus had been born into the rich elegance He deserved, would simple shepherds have been His first worshipers? Not likely. Jesus was born into the simple, everyday world, so He could be the One needed for everyone.

That's the real beauty of Christmas. God's Son come to earth for all of us. That we might all be saved. The message needed a stable instead of a palace. Contrary to current thinking, God has it, but doesn't flaunt it. He didn't give Jesus opulence. He gave Jesus simplicity so we can all embrace Him.

Daily Reflection: Can you take time to enjoy the simplicity of the Christmas story? Is there a decoration or place that causes you to pause and simply rest in the loving gift God gave you? Are there traditions or decorations that pull you away from the simplicity of Christmas?

There's nothing wrong with inflatable snowmen and a tree in every room if that's what you enjoy. But don't let the joy of decorating become the chore of decorating. Don't let them become a distraction from experiencing all God has for you this Christmas.

The Setting—Day Four

Matthew 2:2 "Where is He who has been born King of the Jews? For we saw His star in the east and have come to worship Him."

Every year when they lived at home, we gifted our children an ornament they could take with them when they were grown. This lovely tradition allows each child to take a bit of their childhood with them when they start their own homes and lives.

The year our daughter told us she asked Jesus to forgive her sins and live in her heart, my husband and I chose an ornament to commemorate her choice. The one we picked was a yellow *papier-mâché* star with a Precious Moments nativity scene in the middle because that year, she'd chosen to follow the star to Jesus. True, her star was the Holy Spirit speaking to her heart, but it led her to Jesus all the same.

Because we usually top our tree with an angel, for several years our daughter's ornament was the only star on our tree. While our family decorations may not have always placed a star front and center, I can't deny the importance a star plays in the Christmas story.

A star led the magi from the east on a journey they wouldn't soon forget. With nothing more than prophecies and the star, they packed up and headed out on a long journey to see the new King. Though they were likely learned in star navigation, they still only had a vague sense of where they were going. But they pursued the star confidently. I'm amazed by their dedication. I have trouble navigating with my phone telling me where to go, turn by turn!

I often wonder what this star looked like that these foreign kings recognized it as special and the rest of the world did not. Many have speculated through the years. Some believe God miraculously placed a brand-new star in the sky for this one purpose. Others say it may have been the rare alignment of certain planets combining to create what appeared to be a brighter, new star in the sky.

I don't know the right answer. What I do know is that it would take a lot for me to follow a star on a journey to an unknown location. I'm one of those who, try as I might, cannot see the constellations in the sky. All I see is stars, beautiful stars, but just stars.

As incredible as our stars and constellations are, the magi saw something even more beautiful and unimaginable. They witnessed the fulfilment of prophecy. And the sky was their map to finding the King of Kings. In that star, whether it was miraculously created or simply miraculous timing for an astrological event, the magi saw God's invitation. Leave your land. Come and worship the Christ Child.

Daily Reflection: God may not give us a bright new star shining in the heavens every Christmas. But He's given us one in the story of the magi. The star that brought them to see Jesus is an invitation to us as well.

Through considering the star of the magi, God bids us to travel away from the busyness of our daily lives and follow Him to a quiet place where we can find—and worship—Jesus. Is there a special place in your home that beckons you to come spend time worshipping at Christmas?

The Setting—Day Five

Luke 2:6-7 "While they were there, the days were completed for her to give birth. And she gave birth to her firstborn son; and she wrapped Him in cloths, and laid Him in a manger, because there was no room for them in the inn."

I'll never forget the Christmas before I delivered my first son. At one month before his arrival, I had already received many needed items from baby shower gifts. But as I unwrapped my Christmas gifts that year, I noticed a theme.

Nearly all my gifts were for the baby. That's when it hit. Life was changing. In my head that truth was clear but experiencing the shift through the gifts I received made it sink in deep.

A few weeks later, one of those Christmas gifts became a staple of my nightly routine. My in-laws gave us a beautiful wooden rocker. I spent hours in that chair, cuddling my newborn singing him to sleep. Some nights, I may even have dozed while waiting for his tired eyes to drift closed.

Mary didn't have the luxury of a rocking chair to soothe Jesus's newborn cries. I imagine she held Him close and sang to Him the songs passed down through generations. As his eyes grew heavy and his breathing evened out, Mary gently laid her baby, the Son of God, the Savior of the world, in a manger for his bed.

A manger. Like the stable, we often have a romanticized idea of what this was. We know it's a feeding trough, probably filled with hay for whatever animals usually fed there. But in most nativity sets, we see a carefully constructed wooden box lifted from the ground on legs.

Could baby Jesus's makeshift bed have been made of wood? It's possible. But more likely for the time was a trough constructed of clay and straw. Alternately, His manger could have been carved out of stone, with the middle chiseled out to craft a well to hold food.

As we consider this substitute bed, we realize no matter the material, there is deeper meaning. The manger was an ordinary object, something accessible to all. But it's more than that. The manger was a place of nourishment, of life-giving sustenance.

Do you think Mary realized as she placed baby Jesus in the manger that one day He would tell His disciples, "For the bread of God is that which comes down out of heaven, and gives life to the world ... I am the bread of life; he who comes to Me will not hunger, and he who believes in my will never thirst" (John 6:33 and 35)?

Do you think after watching her son crucified Mary could partake of the Passover meal without Jesus's words, "This is My body which is given for you; do this in remembrance of Me" taking on a deeper meaning? As Mary considered her Son's sacrifice, might her mind have returned to the times she laid Jesus in a manger meant to feed animals when all the time He was the Bread of Life bringing life for all?

Daily Reflection: Mary was given a gift we can only imagine. How rich was her understanding of Jesus's life and God's plan as she watched Him grow and minister? But that gift came with a weight I wouldn't want, knowing her baby would one day die on the cross to provide life. Consider the traditions you enjoy during the Christmas season. Do any of them cause you to stop and reflect on the baby in the manger? How do you acknowledge the Bread of Life broken to give us life?

Reflecting on the Setting

The place God chose as the birthplace of Jesus means something in His story. It shows what God considered important, placing the focus on the person of Jesus and not special birthrights of the privileged or what He owned. Jesus came into a setting every man could relate to in order to become the Savior for every man.

What we surround ourselves with at Christmas can help us to focus our attention on Jesus, remember family and traditions, and create an environment that fosters peace and joy. What are some of your favorite memories that have to do with the setting of your past Christmases?

_____
_____
_____
_____
_____
_____
_____

Is there something you do each year or put out each year that brings you a sense of wonder, peace, or joy?

_____
_____
_____
_____
_____
_____
_____

Is there something that reminds you of the real meaning of Christmas and encourages you to meditate on Jesus?

_____
_____
_____
_____
_____
_____
_____

If you could only pass down one item or tradition related to the setting of your Christmases to your family, what would it be and why?

_____
_____
_____
_____
_____
_____
_____

REFLECTING ON CHRISTMAS PAST

Consider ways you can inspire peace, joy, and wonder for the birth of Jesus through the atmosphere of your home. Write your ideas below.

_____
_____
_____
_____
_____
_____
_____
_____

Be intentional about finding time to enjoy your surroundings this Christmas. While not everything has to be directly related to the birth of Jesus, give yourself a place that draws your attention to Him and take time to meditate on Him in that space.

The People

The People—Day One

Luke 1:26-27 "Now in the sixth month the angel Gabriel was sent from God to a city in Galilee called Nazareth, to a virgin engaged to a man whose name was Joseph, of the descendants of David; and the virgin's name was Mary."

While I'll never forget the childlike angel tree topper with strawberry blonde curls at my parent's house, she wasn't a beautiful heirloom to be passed down through generations. She was cute in a "not really" sort of way, like a child's doll that had a mid-life crisis and changed professions.

She didn't look like she belonged at the top of our tree or any other tree. Her hair made her look like a washed-out Little Orphan Annie. Her plain white gown with a simple red ribbon bow at the neck belonged in a bedtime scene from Little House on the Prairie. There was nothing regal or angelic about her.

Our angel had one thing going for her though. Her superpower left us perplexed, amused, and irritated all at the same time. She blinked off and on. I know what you're thinking. Lots of tree toppers blink. Not like this little angel, I assure you.

It started slow and predictable, as one expects from a Christmas angel. But before long, the light pulses came in rapid succession, then slowed, then sped up again. There was no distinguishable pattern.

Once we adjusted to this strange feature of our angel, she became part of our Christmas tradition. I have to admit, though, I've always wanted to learn Morse Code to see if she had some secret message for us that we missed all these years.

Thankfully, Mary didn't need a translator for her angelic message. Gabriel brought it to her with clarity and confidence. But then, it wasn't Gabriel's first time delivering God's message.

Gabriel spoke with Daniel many years earlier. He brought understanding to Daniel about a disturbing vision Daniel had. Even then, Gabriel announced the coming Messiah.

Only a few months prior to his speaking with Mary, Gabriel brought a message to Zechariah. While Gabriel shared information about Zechariah and Elizabeth's child, it's interesting that, once again, Gabriel shared the news of the coming Messiah.

Did all of Gabriel's earthly messages include an announcement of Jesus's coming? We don't know. Scripture only names two angels, Gabriel and Michael. Other angelic messages were delivered by nameless angels of the Lord. And I can find no other passages where an angel announces the first coming of Jesus. Gabriel fills that purpose when he speaks with Daniel, Zechariah, and Mary.

The secret message of my family's spastic blinking angel was a product of my active imagination. Gabriel's message was true and spoken clearly to those who needed to hear of the coming Savior. Our message today is different.

Ours isn't to speak of a Savior who hasn't arrived yet. We rejoice over the Savior who came, lived, died, and rose again to offer us forgiveness from our sins and reconcile us with God. The gift has been given. The Child has been born. This is our message to proclaim each Christmas.

Daily Reflection: What person, decoration, or song encourages you to reflect on Gabriel's message of the coming Savior and what His coming means for you? Gabriel shared the news with those who needed to hear it. Are there friends, co-workers, and loved ones who need to hear the message that the Savior came, lived, died, and rose again for them? Consider how you might be the messenger God would use to share the truth with them this Christmas.

The People—Day Two

Luke 2:8-9 "In the same region there were some shepherds staying out in the fields and keeping watch over their flock by night. And an angel of the Lord suddenly stood before them, and the glory of the Lord shone around them; and they were terribly frightened."

We didn't camp at our house. But one Christmas an idea took root for a special camping experience for our boys. While we were only able to enjoy it a couple of times before they grew out of the desire, it's one of my treasured Christmas memories.

I'm not sure if my plan was sparked from hearing about Martin Luther as the originator of the Christmas tree. I remember reading about him walking on a winter night, seeing stars twinkling through tree branches. Inspired, it's reported he brought a tree inside and decorated it with candles, bringing the beauty of nature into his home.

The idea of being moved by God's creation may have prompted my Christmas camp-out. Living in southern Illinois, camping outside where we could look at the stars was out of the question.

Instead, I placed pillows and sleeping bags under the branches of our Christmas tree. After an evening of Christmas movies, the boys readied for bed. I turned off all the lights, except for the tree. Looking up through the branches, they watched the twinkling "stars" until they drifted to sleep.

What a peaceful night. I wonder if that's how the shepherds felt in Bethlehem watching sheep outside under the stars. From different accounts I've read, shepherds stayed with flocks through the nights from spring through fall, especially during birthing season. This allowed them to protect and care for newborn lambs.

Maybe the shepherds dealt with birthing lambs that night. Maybe not. Whatever happened, I imagine they regularly looked into the starry expanse as the nights passed. Like us, I'm guessing they discussed the stars' brightness, commented on shooting stars, and were wowed by the beauty of the moon.

Can you imagine how they felt the night Jesus was born? They were accustomed to a beautiful night sky. This time, they looked up and found an angel lighting up the night. They'd never seen this before and never would again. But God wasn't finished wowing them.

After delivering news of the Savior's birth, a multitude of angels joined the first. Angels. Praising God. A message from God. The birth of the long-awaited Savior. How awesome.

The shepherds knew their place in society wasn't one of prestige. Yet, God gave this message to them. God could've arranged for the magi to arrive on the night of Jesus's birth. They could have been first to worship the newborn King.

But Jesus's first worshipers were everyday men, like you and me. They weren't men of importance seeking a king. They were men in need of a Savior. After the angels' message, the shepherds became men of action, leaving the fields to find the baby. They worshiped Him. Then, they spread the news of His arrival so all could know the Savior had come.

Daily Reflection: Angels delivered a message of hope to shepherds. The shepherds sought the Savior. They worshiped and shared joy and hope with everyone.

We've been given the same message. The Savior has come. He gave His life to offer us forgiveness and reconcile us with God. How do you seek the Savior during the weeks leading up to Christmas? What makes you ponder what Jesus's coming means? How do you share that with others?

The People—Day Three

Matthew 1:19-20 and 24 "And Joseph her husband, being a righteous man and not wanting to disgrace her, planned to send her away secretly. But when he had considered this, behold, an angel of the Lord appeared to him in a dream, saying, 'Joseph, son of David, do not be afraid to take Mary as your wife; for the Child who has been conceived in her is of the Holy Spirit.' And Joseph awoke from his sleep and did as the angel of the Lord commanded him and took Mary as his wife."

The DuQuoin State Fairgrounds host a yearly Christmas lights display. When my children were younger, they loved the whimsical displays. Inside the Expo Hall, crafters and vendors set up shop. Musicians played. Children laughed as they played games, made ornaments, and rode the small train. Cameras flashed at children on Santa's lap.

My boys grew out of this tradition, but I still loved the lights. The last year we went, I begged my kids to come as a birthday gift to me. Wrong choice.

They went. We looked at the lights. Then, we visited the Expo Hall. My mom offered to take a family picture. My boys were not feeling it.

Beside the smiling faces of my husband and myself are three less than thrilled expressions. My oldest son tried to fake a smile, resulting in a grimace worthy of any awkward school photo. Though he hadn't hit the teens, my middle son's expression is the barely there tolerance every teen wears as a teacher gives them a detention for their attitude. The youngest? Empty. Like a juvenile mug shot.

My sons didn't want to attend the display that year. Disdain showed in each face and attitude. Aren't we often that way when life brings us something we don't want?

Joseph had more reason than most for a bad attitude leading up to that first Christmas. His fiancée was expecting, and he wasn't the father. She'd wronged him, but he loved her. He wouldn't make an example out of her as allowed by law, but he wasn't marrying her either.

With this decision, the truth came to light. An angel visited Joseph in a dream. The messenger assured Joseph that Mary had done no wrong. She carried the Son of God, and Joseph shouldn't fear taking Mary as his wife.

Learning of Mary's faithfulness probably brought relief, but the truth wasn't what Joseph expected for his life. He would marry a woman who society, their friends, and family, would always whisper about. Imagine the rolled eyes and derogatory statements from non-believing neighbors at Mary's claim of innocence. Or more unbelievable, that the Child was the Son of God sent to save them?

Joseph had reason for a less than cheerful attitude and complaining. He could have begrudgingly done God's will. Mary and Jesus could've been treated like second-class citizens in their own home due to bitterness at his situation.

We don't have reason to believe any of those attitudes had a place in Joseph's heart. What we do see is care and concern for Mary and Jesus. Scripture tells us he woke and did as God asked. Joseph was a righteous man. God led. Joseph followed.

Daily Reflection: Joseph could've chosen disobedience or begrudging obedience. Instead, he followed with an obedient heart. At Christmas, do you struggle with having a positive attitude? Is God asking you to trust Him and continue in those situations that challenge you? Pray for wisdom to know which to step away from and a righteous attitude for those He asks you to continue.

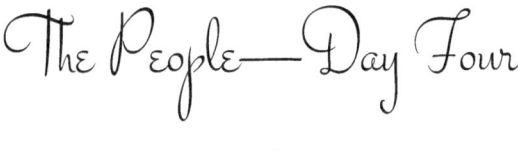

Luke 1:39-42 "Now at this time Mary arose and went in a hurry to the hill country, to a city of Judah, and entered the house of Zacharias and greeted Elizabeth. When Elizabeth heard Mary's greeting, the baby leaped in her womb; and Elizabeth was filled with the Holy Spirit. And she cried out with a loud voice and said, 'Blessed are you among women, and blessed is the fruit of your womb!'

Holiday celebrations can be tough for introverts. With friends and family to visit, Christmas can wear out an introvert's last nerve. Even worse, Christmas is sandwiched between Thanksgiving and New Year's Eve, also people-heavy holidays.

Do you thrive on interaction? Then you may not see the problem. But for those who desire peace, calm, and silence the holidays can feel more like chaos than comfort and joy. When the family introvert is responsible for the family game-plan, stress can overflow.

Noise, lights, events, and people overwhelm. The one who needs calm and time alone to recharge becomes anxious, exhausted, and stressed. Even drama-free, fun get-togethers can create the need to stay outside it all or even temporarily escape.

Just because the introverts don't join in every event or fully integrate into the crowd, it doesn't mean they're not having fun. Their actions aren't a sign they're angry, frustrated, or disappointed. They may be attempting to avoid those feelings.

Give your introvert one-to-one time and downtime. Escaping the crowd doesn't mean they're running from you or the family. They simply need the time to recharge.

Was Mary an introvert? We're not told. In fact, Scripture doesn't tell us her hometown even knew of her pregnancy. However, knowing the human propensity for gossip, the news would have traveled quickly from house to house. Even if they didn't know immediately, a few months into her pregnancy, the truth would be apparent. Introvert or extrovert that kind of attention wouldn't be welcome. No one, not even those who love people and attention, want everyone's focus as "that" person in town.

We do know, early in her pregnancy, Mary visited her cousin Elizabeth who was also expecting. As Mary arrived, Elizabeth's unborn baby reacted to Jesus's presence. While that would be amazing, I believe Elizabeth's reaction would have meant even more to Mary.

Mary. Facing an unexpected pregnancy and the doubts and fears any new mother faces. Mary. Who knew her child was the Son of God. Mary. Who wondered if Joseph might break their engagement and heard whispers calling her crazy or a liar or both.

When she arrived at Elizabeth's home, away from the crowds and the whispers, her cousin did a wonderful thing. She cut through the fears and doubts to speak truth, "Blessed are you among women and blessed is the fruit of your womb."

Can you imagine Mary's relief? Her cousin understood and cheered her on. Elizabeth took her in. Further into her own pregnancy, Elizabeth would have been a mentor, teaching Mary what to expect.

Scripture doesn't tell us everything that happened, either in Mary's mind or throughout her visit with Elizabeth. But it doesn't take much imagination to understand the issues Mary might have struggled with or how visiting Elizabeth freed her spirit to sing her beautiful song of praise (Luke 1: 46-55).

Daily Reflection: Mary needed support and encouragement. She found both in a trusted friend. Consider which of your friendships provide support and encouragement for you during Christmas. What holiday plans include those people? Which activities add to the noise and which ones reduce your stress? How can you be an Elizabeth to your friends this Christmas?

Isaiah 9:7 "There will be no end to the increase of His government or of peace, on the throne of David and over his kingdom, To establish it and to uphold it with justice and righteousness from then on and forevermore, the zeal of the LORD of hosts will accomplish this."

"You won't tell your dad what we got him, right?"

My young daughter dutifully shook her head every time. "Oh, no," she said. "I won't tell. It's a secret."

Here's a secret: Surprises didn't stay surprises long when my daughter was around. It happened every year. Sometimes more than once. It became a family joke. No one ever Christmas-shopped with her. At least, not if they wanted their gifts to remain a surprise.

Her intentions were good. She *wanted* to keep the secrets. But the anticipation of the receiver's surprise and delight over their gifts was too much.

"Do you know what we got today, Daddy?"

After a few times, Daddy learned to answer her question with one of his own. "Was it a Christmas present for me? If so, remember, you aren't supposed to tell."

Reminders help. A little. Waiting is hard. Especially when you know your gift is one the other person will love.

God knows about anticipation. He created mankind in His image. Nothing else in creation claimed that same relationship with its Creator. With Adam and Eve's sin in the garden, God felt the loss of fellowship with His prized creation. The physical and spiritual death resulting from sin destroyed the intimacy between God and man. Their daily walks together through the garden ended. Sin stole that pleasure from God.

But God wasn't done with His creation. In His great love for and desire to be with us, He determined to bridge the gap we could never cross on our own. His plan would satisfy sin's requirement of death. Though the priced demanded was steep, God was willing to pay it to redeem His creation.

Immanuel, God with us, meant canceling sin's debt for all who would accept Jesus's death as the substitute for their own. Jesus's life, death, and resurrection aren't just a good gift. They're the perfect gift for every one of us. And God was excited to see His gift become a reality.

Isaiah 9:7 uses the word zeal to describe how God felt about His plan to reconcile with us. Zeal. It's a powerful word. Zeal suggests words like passionate enthusiasm, uncontainable anticipation, and fierce determination to do accomplish whatever you're zealous for.

This word, with all it means, was chosen by God to describe His feelings about offering us the salvation we so desperately need. It paints a picture of God's growing excitement for His reconciliation with His creation—our return to an intimate relationship with Him.

Daily Reflection: Christmas reminds us that God values relationships. Ours with Him and ours with others. Reconnect with God this Christmas season. Ask Him to show you how to reconnect with friends and family as well. With the busyness of the season, it can feel like yet another chore to spend time with everyone. Which past activities did you look forward to that also fostered real connection with your loved ones? Are those still part of your holiday? Ask God to show you if they should be or if He has another way for you to connect that you can look forward to with enthusiasm.

Reflecting on the People

Christmas often means extended periods of time with family and friends. As wonderful as this is, it can also be difficult. There's often conflict over differences. Other times loss leaves those who remain feeling more abandoned than before. The pressure we can feel to make everything perfect for friends and family can rob us of our enjoyment of the celebration. But would the Christmas season be the same without those we love, even those who challenge us?

Think back through your most cherished Christmases. Who are the people that shared those times with you?

_____
_____
_____
_____
_____
_____
_____

Why were those Christmases special to you?

_____
_____
_____
_____
_____
_____

Some people need time alone to recharge during the holidays. For some of us, this is essential to our emotional well-being. However, the temptation can be to turn down every invitation to celebrate the season with others. What are some ways you can find the balance between taking care of your need for solitude and spending time with those you love?

_____
_____
_____
_____
_____
_____

Christmas can be a hard time for many. Those who have lost loved ones or who live solitary lives due to age or infirmity, or those who are dealing with other disappointing life changes such as military deployment, divorce, or other separation, can all find it hard to remember there is something to celebrate.

Even those of us who aren't struggling with hard times can find ourselves fighting depression and anxiety in the often-demanding times of the holidays. When we're focused on self it is hard to see past whatever is pulling us down. What are some practical ways you could be

REFLECTING ON CHRISTMAS PAST

intentional about reaching out to those in need this Christmas? If you are the one suffering, what could someone else do to ease your pain?

_____
_____
_____
_____
_____
_____
_____
_____

Helping others is a powerful way to change not only their experience but also your own perspective. Connecting with others during the Christmas season reminds us of the meaning of Christmas. After all, Jesus is God *with* us. From birth to death His life was about giving us freedom from sin.

THE SOUNDS

The Sounds—Day One

Luke 2:8-14 *"In the same region there were some shepherds staying out in the fields and keeping watch over their flocks by night. And an angel of the Lord suddenly stood before them, and the glory of the Lord shone around them; and they were terribly frightened. But the angel said to them, 'Do not be afraid; for behold, I bring you good news of great joy which will be for all people; for today in the city of David there has been born for you a Savior, who is Christ the Lord. This will be a sign for you: you will find a baby wrapped in cloths and lying in a manger.' And suddenly there appeared with the angel a multitude of the heavenly host praising God and saying, 'Glory to God in the highest, And on earth peace among men with whom He is pleased.'"*

Which sounds calm you at Christmas? For me it's "Christmas Canon" by Trans-Siberian Orchestra. When the programs, services, parties, and minute details of Christmas create unease, this song soothes me. Whether the chaos comes in trying to budget money that isn't there or I can't wrangle my kids into one place long enough to decorate the tree, my frayed nerves still when this song plays.

I don't know why. There's no emotional connection and it doesn't overflow with spiritual meaning. But each time it instantly transforms my mood, calming my spirit. Not even the classical base melody accomplishes that. The calm only comes in listening to this version.

Sounds affect us. And not just music. A rainstorm may incite fear or relaxation. Some find waves crashing on the beach calming. Wind blowing through leaves speaks peace to others. Sounds can bring anxiety, calm, inspiration, or excitement.

The shepherds in these verses understood this. Seeing an angel, they were afraid. His words, "Do not be afraid," were meant to calm so they could hear the message. Once the message was delivered, the sky filled with a host of heavenly angels. Imagine the sight! If one angel frightened the shepherds, I'm not sure a host would have ushered in peace. But they weren't only seen. The angels also made themselves heard.

We like to envision an angel choir singing the "Hallelujah Chorus" in perfect harmony. We imagine a song more beautiful than man can create. But Scripture doesn't tell us they sang. It says they praised God and *spoke*. While a beautiful song could have accompanied their praise, their message, even if spoken, is still amazing.

Though without a specific number, a host of angels is a group of great magnitude. This wasn't a small gathering of angels. It wasn't a select few of heaven's best announcers. This was a host, a multitude.

Singing or not, imagine the sound of the heavenly host as in unison they proclaimed, "Glory to God in the highest." What a sound to fill the hillside! The message and method inspired the shepherds' trek to find Jesus. Moved by what they heard, they immediately made their way to the manger. They added their own voices of worship to the sounds of heaven.

Daily Reflection: What sounds usher in a sense of peace and well-being for you? Do you take the respite offered to meditate on God's gift of Jesus? Whether your peace is in a children's choir, a yearly concert, the laughter of your family playing games, or a single song, do you let the sound create a calming pause? This Christmas be intentional in seeking this sound. Take advantage of it. Let God's peace wash over you.

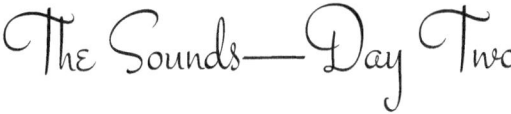

Luke 2:3 and 7 "And everyone was on his way to register for the census, each to his own city. ... And she gave birth to her firstborn son; and she wrapped him in cloths, and laid Him in a manger, because there was no room for them in the inn."

One of the first Christmas songs I learned was "Silent Night." I'm sure it ranks up there with "Away in a Manger" as the top songs performed in children's Christmas programs, but I misunderstood a lot about the song when I was a child.

"Round yon virgin." I was never sure what yon was, but I knew Mary was round because she was pregnant. I thought this line took place before she gave birth and the next one, "Mother and child", showed Jesus finally arrived.

"Glories stream from heaven afar" and "Radiant beams from Thy holy face" were also a little problematic. I had no idea what glories were, just that they came with angels. The radiant beams made me wonder if baby Jesus's face lit up like a night light.

I'm not sure when I finally grasped the real meaning of these lines. Honestly, I still find them a little strange. But at least I understand them now. My childish misunderstandings have been replaced with new questions, though.

I can't argue against the holiness of the night Jesus was born. Holy means sacred or something set apart for God. The day, hour, and moment Jesus entered our world as a baby were ordained by God. He planned the arrival intentionally, for our eternal benefit, making it holy.

But silent? People filled the town of Bethlehem to capacity. While some walked, others would have brought livestock with them. Add additional people and animals to those who made their homes in Bethlehem, and the noise level increases.

We're not told Jesus's birth stats. We don't know what time of night He arrived, how much He weighed or what His length was. We simply know it was night and there was some level of darkness since angels lit up the sky. But it is possible people were still awake when Jesus was born.

We do know the shepherds went around telling everyone what happened. Were they at the manger for hours before announcing His arrival to the rest of the town or did they knock on doors in the middle of the night spreading the news?

There are many details we don't have regarding Jesus's birth. But unless God intervened, I can't see how the night was silent. Did the author of the carol take creative license? Almost certainly. But maybe not as much as we imagine.

The lyrics create a picture of peacefulness, perfection. Upon His arrival, the Prince of Peace began His journey to provide peace between us and God. Whatever noises were present physically the night Jesus was born, perfection and peace arrived. They were lying in the manger.

Perfection and peace. An end to the chaos of sin. Spiritual stillness as our hearts are made right with God. Maybe "silent night" is right, after all.

Daily Reflection: Do you struggle to accept the postcard worthy nativity scene created by song writers? Regardless of the actual details, peace and stillness are found in the coming of Jesus. What traditions, songs, or activities encourage you to meditate on the peace and holiness Jesus brings? Make time for those this Christmas season.

The Sounds—Day Three

Luke 1:46-48 "And Mary said: 'My soul exalts the Lord, and my spirit has rejoiced in God my Savior. For He has had regard for the humble state of His bondslave; For behold, from this time on all generations will count me blessed."

In 1992, Amy Grant released a song on her Christmas album that is still sung and played today. "Breath of Heaven" explores what might have been going through Mary's mind as she brought God's Son into the world.

The melody is haunting and powerful, as are the words. It makes sense that Mary, as young as it's believed she was, would wonder why God chose her for this task. I'd question it too. And it stands to reason that her unique situation combined with the strict moral code of her people might make her feel a bit alone in a time when she needed support the most. And it isn't a stretch to think Mary knew she needed God's strength to help her through.

The prayer that serves as the song's chorus is one many of us could pray as we face uncertain circumstances or feel led from our comfort zones. In the song, Mary asks God to hold her and to be near her forever. I can imagine Mary's heart pouring out those words to her God.

Of course, we don't have record of every thought Mary entertained during her pregnancy and the birth of Jesus. But Luke 1 gives us great insight into the mindset of Mary, at least on a day when she was welcomed by family and encouraged by her cousin's faithful response to her news.

On that day, Mary praised God. Her heart overflowed with thankfulness for God's plan at work in her life. Whether she faced hard times from those around her or not, during this time, Mary realized the privilege of being chosen for this part in God's salvation story. All women would call her blessed. She was blessed.

Mary offered praise not only for her part in God's plan, but for God's provision and grace and mercy throughout the history of her people. The entire plan didn't have to be laid out for her in detail before she could accept her place and give God praise. Mary had seen God's faithfulness firsthand and through the stories of faith she grew up on. Everything didn't have to be perfect with everyone accepting the truth before Mary could believe God's plan for her was good.

She looked at the past and knew the truth by faith.

Looking at her heritage of faith gave Mary the strength to not only accept her part in God's plan but to embrace it with a heart full of praise.

Daily Reflection: We will never know in this life everything Mary dealt with during her pregnancy and Jesus's birth. But we know the stories of faith she heard through her life enabled her to move forward in eager anticipation of her part in God's plan.

Reflect on the stories of God's love and faithfulness at Christmas that you've heard through the years. Do you have any traditions that reinforce these stories? Do you have a way to pass them on to your loved ones each year? This year, allow the truths you've heard to open your heart, and praise God for your part in His plan.

The Sounds—Day Four

Isaiah 40:3 "A voice is calling, 'Clear the way for the LORD in the wilderness; Make smooth in the desert a highway for our God.'"

There are many great traditional Christmas songs, some going back hundreds of years. There's a song for every mood. Fun and childlike. Serious. Reflective. Even worshipful.

A beautiful one I never heard growing up is "I Heard the Bells on Christmas Day." The song's message is beautiful. It evokes images of peaceful melodies ringing through the crisp morning air, inviting those who hear them to come worship the Christ-child.

I'm not sure why this song wasn't sung more often. Maybe, it's because many have never heard bells ringing in Christmas Day. The churches where I live never ring out on Christmas. I'm not sure how many even have bells anymore.

While they aren't church bells and they don't ring on Christmas Day, other bells have ushered in the Christmas season in my life through the years. Growing up, the men and women collecting for the Salvation Army positioned themselves outside of many stores with their red kettles and their bells.

As I reached adulthood, if I needed to visit multiple stores, I tried to remember to take a handful of change with me. If I forgot, I inevitably felt bad that I couldn't give to each person. I knew in my head, it all went to the same place, but those individuals were out giving of themselves in the cold. I wanted each one to experience that encouragement.

These days, I don't hear or see those bell ringers as often as I once did—and that makes me sad. Every time I heard those bells ringing, I knew Christmas was coming. The message of goodwill to men echoed in every ring, encouraging passersby to reach out in love to those in need. A handful of change could make a difference in someone's life.

John the Baptist is the bellringer for Jesus. Born before Him, and not actually present in the Christmas story, nevertheless, his life was spent ushering in the real meaning of Christmas. He proclaimed "God with us" and that the gift of salvation is available to all. It wasn't his job. It was his life and who he was at his core.

God made man. Jesus deserved a herald to pave the way for His ministry. We needed that pronouncement that the time had come. On the night Jesus was born, the angelic message filled the night air. Then, as Jesus prepared to step into His ministry on this earth, John took up their song. Whether through the heavenly host or that single man, the message rang out as clearly as the bells on Christmas day.

Daily Reflection: What events, traditions, songs, or Scriptures have helped prepare your heart for past Christmases? Have you made those part of your Christmas this year? The message isn't for us alone. We can be the heavenly host, John the Baptist, and the bellringers for others as we declare the need to make room for Jesus and the gift of salvation set in motion with His birth. How can you let the truth in your heart ring out to those you love this Christmas season?

Luke 1:41 "When Elizabeth heard Mary's greeting, the baby leaped in her womb; and Elizabeth was filled with the Holy Spirit."

As children, we didn't have to drum up excitement at Christmas. Beautiful, colorful decorations not only filled our homes, but also our yards and every store. We heard songs reserved only for this special time of year. Fun movies we loved were shown as the time drew close. Winter break from school further encouraged our joy.

We had plenty of reasons as children to get excited for Christmas, and we didn't even have to mention the tree surrounded by gifts.

Sometimes, adulthood steals the joy of Christmas. Instead of taking pleasure in all those things that brought us delight as children, we're faced with the impossible tasks of working out holiday schedules or fighting crowds at the mall for the best deals on the hottest gifts. Our to-do list is maxed out with house-cleaning chores before our family descends like vultures to devour, in minutes, the meal it took us hours to prepare.

We get caught up in these things and lose sight of the one reason we should always be excited for Christmas. John acknowledged it before he was even born, and it poured over into his mother, Elizabeth.

When John heard Mary's voice, that's all it took. He responded with enthusiasm. Scripture doesn't tell us John kicked in his mother's womb or turned over. It says the baby leaped inside her. The wording creates an image of the baby inside engaged in a flurry of excited movement at the arrival of Jesus into his home.

But the unborn John was not the only one affected. His mother, Elizabeth, wasn't left unchanged. After Mary's greeting and after experiencing John's reaction, Elizabeth was filled with the Holy Spirit. She greeted Mary with elation, crying out in joy and praise for what God was doing through her.

There were no wreaths hung on their doors. No lights strung on a tree. "Silent Night" did not play, and no special meal was being prepared. In fact, life went on—with the normal obligations and expectations. What changed was the people.

John and Elizabeth recognized the arrival of the one person whose presence provided reason to celebrate. Their focus on the gift of Jesus was more than enough to fill them with anticipation and joy.

Did you catch that? They didn't need the decorations and carefree days of childhood to rejoice at Christmas—and neither do we. Furthermore, the responsibilities we carry as adults don't have to steal our joy or our eager anticipation of the season.

All we need to do, like John and Elizabeth, is adjust our focus. We need to set our minds and hearts on the one person who gives Christmas its meaning. We need to listen for and anticipate Him as we prepare for the holiday.

Jesus. The only begotten Son, Lamb of God, Bread of Life, Redeemer. Our Prince of Peace, King of Kings, Savior. Immanuel, God with us.

He's the one person we need at our Christmas celebration. It's His voice we need to hear above all else to usher in the excitement of the Christmas season.

Daily Reflection: Does dread or excitement fill your days as Christmas approaches? Consider the activities and demands on your time during the holidays. Do those things invite Jesus into your celebration or keep you from welcoming Him? What helps you hear Jesus above all the other sounds clamoring for your attention? What could enable your excitement to grow and overflow as you listen to His voice this Christmas?

Reflecting on the Sounds

I love Christmas music, from silly children's songs to meaning-filled religious songs. Some lift my spirits and some turn me nostalgic. There are some that tug at my heart and coax a few tears from my eyes whenever I hear them.

But I also love the sound of my children laughing together while decorating the Christmas tree and the spirited discussions around the table during Christmas dinner. And though I don't hear them as often as I once did, I still love the sound of the Salvation Army bell ringers seeking help for those less fortunate.

Think about the sounds you've heard through the years at Christmas. What is one that stands out to you?

_____
_____
_____
_____
_____
_____

Is there a Christmas song that always impacts you in a positive way? What do you love about this particular song?

_____
_____
_____
_____
_____
_____
_____

I imagine the angels praising God in the starry night was a sound the shepherds never forgot. It pointed them to Jesus, and they responded by worshipping Him. What sounds cause you to focus on the real meaning of Christmas?

_____
_____
_____
_____
_____
_____
_____

Read Luke 2:16-18. After hearing the angels and finding the baby in the manger, the shepherds added their own voice to the wonder and praise of Christmas. How can you do the same this year?

_____
_____
_____
_____
_____

REFLECTING ON CHRISTMAS PAST

_____
_____

What are some ways you can surround yourself with sounds of Christmas that will encourage you to reflect on the good news the angels proclaimed on that hillside?

_____
_____
_____
_____
_____
_____
_____
_____

The sounds we hear have powerful effects in our lives. Be intentional about filling your space with sounds that encourage you this season.

THE GIFT

The Gift—Day One

Matthew 2:11 *"After coming into the house they saw the Child with Mary His mother; and they fell to the ground and worshiped Him. Then, opening their treasures, they presented to Him gifts of gold, frankincense, and myrrh."*

One of my most treasured gifts came from my husband. Before I was ever a published author, I knew God had placed the dream of writing in my heart. I'd attended conferences, made connections, and grown in the craft. Still, I remained unpublished. I felt defeated.

Then Andy surprised me with registration to a small writer's conference. My favorite author was presenting. My prayer was to do for others in writing what her stories did for me. And Andy provided this opportunity to meet and learn from her.

I attended workshops and met my writing hero. She signed my favorite book of hers. I had a one-on-one session with her, and we continued talking as we ate lunch together. It was amazing.

As a reader the experience was unforgettable. As an author, it changed things for me. She spoke about topics I struggled with. It was like God put her there just for me, though I know she also blessed others. Even now, I return to her words of encouragement.

In fact, in many ways, I am still receiving my husband's gift. Well-thought-out gifts touch our lives beyond the moment. Their meaning extends far into our lives. This is the kind of gifting the wise men did.

Traveling many miles to worship a king, their gifts reflected that. Gold, frankincense, and myrrh. Not typical baby gifts. Not a rattle, block, or teether in the lot. But Jesus wasn't just another baby. The magi's gifts honored a long-awaited king.

Did they fully understand the situation? Maybe not. If they had, they probably wouldn't have asked Herod about Jesus's whereabouts. They likely wouldn't have needed to change their route following a dream. Still, God used them to honor Jesus as King and Savior.

The gifts of the first Christmas hold special meaning we can weave into our own celebrations. It's not about the giver or the value of the gifts. Religious symbolism is attached to the gifts. We don't have scriptural proof that God intended this symbolism, but it's not discounted either.

Gold reflects Jesus's kingship. Frankincense is used in worship. The gift of myrrh is associated with death and burial, foreshadowing Jesus's death and resurrection. The true King worthy of worship coming as sacrifice for man. Jesus's true nature and purpose summed up in three gifts.

Do you suppose Mary remembered these gifts at various points in Jesus's life? Did gold and frankincense come to mind as her son rode into Jerusalem on the donkey? As she joined the other women to prepare burial spices after His death, did the myrrh trigger a bittersweet memory of the first time He received the spice? At His resurrection, did the full import of those first gifts become clear?

Despite their symbolism, these gifts aren't the most important ones Jesus received from the Wise Men at His birth. The givers' intent was the true gift. The wise men left home, following the star, so they could *worship the newborn king*. Their gifts were presented to Jesus in honor of who He was.

REFLECTING ON CHRISTMAS PAST

Daily Reflection: Jesus is the same today as He was when the wise men worshiped with their gifts. He is the true King who sacrificed Himself for us. He is worthy of our gift of worship. Consider how you've honored Jesus with your gifts of worship during past Christmases. Was it through special quiet times? Giving your time to help others? Fasting? What can you do this year to ensure you're giving Jesus the gift of your worship as Christmas draws near?

The Gift—Day Two

Matthew 1:23 "'Behold, the virgin shall be with child and shall bear a Son, and they shall call his name Immanuel,' which translated means, 'God with us.'"

As a child, I received a gift I still have today. As far as gifts are concerned, it isn't anything especially valuable or useful. At least, I don't think Chubbles are worth anything. How could they be? They're a stuffed animal resembling a generic Ewok wearing a cloak.

The claim to fame for a Chubble is that the three bulbs making up its eyes and nose (there is no mouth) are actually a light bulb and a light sensor. When you cover the sensor eye, the nose blinks and the Chubble trills a happy chirp.

It's a silly thing, really. But I've kept it for more than thirty years. Why? Because my father gave it to me.

My mom did the Christmas shopping at our house. But that year, my dad decided to buy one gift for each of us kids on his own. Mom didn't go with him. She didn't give him ideas. My brothers and I sure didn't give him a Christmas wish list, because we didn't even know he was doing it.

It's amazing how much worth can be given to something so ordinary simply because of the one who did the giving.

Jesus's birth is the starting point of God's greatest gift to mankind, and He came wrapped in cloths in a manger. Ordinary and unremarkable on the surface, like my father's gift to me, but made infinitely valuable when we consider the One who gifted Jesus to us and what He actually offers us.

God is our Creator. He is holy and good and worthy of our gifts of worship. God is the one we wrong with our sin. He's the one we fail over and over again as we chose self over Him. Yet He loves us and desires relationship with us so much that He chose to gift us with the one thing we could never provide for ourselves. Salvation.

Salvation is a gift from God. It is nothing we earn or supply on our own. Without Jesus's birth there would be no death and resurrection, no salvation. We would be left to pay the price of our sin on our own through eternal separation from God. Jesus's birth ushered in God's amazing gift to us.

Jesus came to earth into an ordinary family, but He is easily the most extraordinary gift we will ever receive. He is God with us.

Jesus gave up heaven, the worship and the power, to become one of us. And since being humbled in this way was not enough to save us, Jesus went all the way to the cross and the grave and then back again so we can have freedom from our sin debt and a renewed relationship with Him.

Without that first Christmas gift of God's Son, there would be no reason to give. There would be no Christmas.

Daily Reflection: Think about the gifts you have received and given. What makes them special? Take time this Christmas to consider the gift of salvation you've been given. What can you do to foster a time for reflecting on God's gift to you and encourage others to do the same?

The Gift—Day Three

James 1:17 "Every good thing given and every perfect gift is from above, coming down from the Father of lights, with whom there is no variation or shifting shadow."

For me, finding the perfect gift is a necessity. I've heard the adage, "It's the thought that counts." But I've gotten some mis-matched gifts that made me wonder what the giver's thoughts toward me actually were. Like giving a peanut butter sandwich to someone with a peanut allergy, the gifts were far removed from my personality, interests, and tastes.

Before I get emails berating me for my ungrateful attitude, I want to assure you, I do understand the real meaning of the saying. And I do respond with gratitude that the giver took time to remember me during the holiday. Care and acts of love from others are always reasons to give thanks.

It is, however, my goal to match up the gifts I give with the one I'm giving them to. This task is easy most of the time, and rewarding. The one exception to this is my father-in-law. He's a quiet man, not given to long or in-depth conversations that might clue me in as to what he would like. Due to physical limitations, he can't enjoy the hobbies he once did. If he has a need or want throughout the year, he typically goes and gets it himself.

I've all but given up on finding the perfect gift for him. I seek my husband's advice, but he's not much help with his shrugs and assurances that he has no more idea than I do what to get his father. The real problem is a lack of understanding on my part of what captures my father-in-law's attention.

I may miss the mark in gift-giving at times. I try, but sometimes, I don't have a clear picture of the one I'm giving to. The gift and the gifted don't match up.

Isn't it reassuring to know that we don't have to worry about whether or not God's gifts to us are going to fit? God's gifts to us are always perfect.

The gifting that started with Jesus's birth on the first Christmas didn't stop there, of course. When Jesus died and rose again to pay the consequence of our sins and offer salvation, it was the greatest gift we will ever be given. But God didn't even stop with that!

God continues to give us His presence in our daily lives. His Spirit living in us teaches us, guides us, and corrects us. We have been gifted the opportunity to participate in sharing His gift of salvation and His love with others. And this is all on top of peace, hope, joy, and even the physical gifts He blesses us with.

Each gift God gives, we know beyond a doubt is perfect for us. God knows us more intimately than we know ourselves. He is aware of our strengths, weaknesses, hopes, failures, and every choice we've ever made or will make. Since He knows us completely and His love is perfect, we have assurance His gifts to us are exactly what we need.

Daily Reflection: How have you celebrated God's gifts to you during past Christmases? Take time to reflect on the gifts, both spiritual and physical, God has given you through the year. How can you celebrate those gifts this Christmas? How might you encourage your loved ones to recognize God's gifts in their lives through sharing your own?

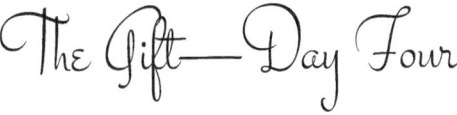

Luke 2:25-30 "And there was a man in Jerusalem whose name was Simeon; and this man was righteous and devout, looking for the consolation of Israel; and the Holy Spirit was upon him. And it had been revealed to him by the Holy Spirit that he would not see death before he had seen the Lord's Christ. And he came in the Spirit into the temple; and when the parents brought in the child Jesus, to carry out for Him the custom of the Law, then he took Him into his arms, and blessed God, and said, 'Now Lord, You are releasing Your bond-servant to depart in peace, According to your word; For my eyes have seen Your salvation..."

As a child, I was always placed near the back row of my class in the yearly Christmas music program. It wasn't because of my singing or my name. We were arranged by height, and I've always been tall for a girl. If all the websites I've seen are correct, my height is taller than the average guy.

On the odd occasion the arrangement placed other students on the highest tiers of the risers, I, without fail, blocked my classmate's ability to see and possibly even kept others from seeing them.

At Christmas parades, I was never the one hoisted onto my parent's shoulders. Even now, and even at the back of the crowd, I rarely need to strain to see the action. The same goes for watching the actors on stage at a Christmas program.

Consequently, I often had the opposite problem. Conscious of those behind me, I sought out ways to make myself smaller. Though it happened frequently, I never wanted to impede another's ability to see the action.

Simeon's height didn't matter when he met Jesus. God gave Simeon a front row seat at Jesus's coming. Due to Simeon's faithfulness, God also gave him a promise: He would not die before seeing the salvation of God.

Can you imagine how it felt when Simeon, after anxiously waiting his whole life, finally saw Jesus come through the door of the temple? In that one child, Simeon saw God's plan to reunite with His people coming to fruition. He saw hope realized. Love and Salvation personified.

Those same things Simeon saw are ours to see now. As we consider Jesus's birth, hope and love are given form. When we look to His death and resurrection, the hope and love solidify into the gift of salvation God offers each of us.

We see it laid out for us in Scripture. When we accept God's gift of salvation through Jesus, we're able to see it more clearly as God's Spirit takes up residence in our hearts. As the Holy Spirit grows us, we see more and more of Jesus. We don't have to worry about whether or not we'll be able to see Him. Because, like He did for Simeon, God gives us a front row seat to see Himself.

Daily Reflection: Christmas is a wonderful time to see Jesus all around us. Reflect on how God has revealed Himself to you through past Christmases. How can you look for Jesus this season? Are there ways you can help ensure others see Him through you?

Luke 2:15-16 "When the angels had gone away from them into heaven, the shepherds began saying to one another, 'Let us go straight to Bethlehem then, and see this thing that has happened which the Lord has made known to us.' So they came in a hurry and found their way to Mary and Joseph, and the baby as He lay in the manger."

"We're serious. Don't get us anything."

It's a sentiment my parents have shared with me since I started earning my own income. The idea was then echoed by my in-laws from the time my husband and I married. Whether it's because I'm paying for school, paying for a child, or paying for a child's school, their reasoning is clear. They feel I should forgo buying gifts for them in order to use that money for other things.

Imagine my surprise when I surveyed the circumstances of my own children and found the words, "We're serious. You don't need to get us anything," coming out of my mouth.

I love gifts.

I love giving gifts most of all. (I won't pretend I don't enjoy receiving them too. I do.) But even better than a pretty package under the tree with my name on it is having all my children and grandchildren show up to spend time with me and my husband on Christmas day. With adult work schedules and visitation with the other set of parents to work out, getting all my children and their children gathered at the same time is close to a Christmas miracle.

Even if it's not all at the same time, I still cherish the time I get to spend with each one. And as much as I enjoy having the whole group together, sometimes I get even better-quality time with them if they come one by one. So, whether they come together or individually, with or without packages, their presence is the greatest gift they have to give me.

Reading the Christmas story, I'm glad the shepherds and the wise men didn't arrive to meet Jesus at the same time. Without the wealthy kings and their fancy presents distracting them, the shepherds weren't tempted to look at anyone or anything other than the Son of God sent to save them. Their bodies, minds, and hearts were solely focused on Jesus.

When Mary looked back at the miraculous birth of her son, I'm sure the wise men came to mind. They were part of His story with their lengthy travel and gifts of gold, frankincense, and myrrh. But I don't believe she treasured their treasures any more than the gift she received from the simple shepherds on the night of Jesus's birth.

You don't recall the shepherds bringing any gifts? While they may not have brought her trinkets and treasures, the shepherds did bring an amazing gift. They brought the news of heralding angels. They left their fields, their livelihoods, to seek out the Good Shepherd. Pure and singularly-focused worship of the Savior was ushered into the stable with the shepherds' arrival. And that was enough for Mary to "treasure all these things, pondering them in her heart." (Luke 2:19)

Daily Reflection: Being with the ones I love, without distraction, is the greatest gift my children can give me. For Mary, the gift of worship the shepherds offered was as cherished as the treasures of kings.

What has drawn you into God's presence with worship during previous Christmas seasons? How can you foster that spirit of fellowship and worship in your celebrations this year? Remember to offer God the present of your presence at the manger, just as the shepherds did many years ago.

Reflecting on the Gifts

I'm a gift-giver. I love to find the perfect gift for each person on my list. I want my gifts to show I've thought about each one specifically and taken time to choose something I hope will have meaning to them. Giving the quick and easy gift is sometimes necessary, but it rarely feels as good to me as when I tailor the gift to the one who receives it. Gifts should mean something.

Is there a gift you've received from family or a friend that means more to you than any other? Why is it special?

_____
_____
_____
_____
_____
_____
_____
_____

Have you ever given the "perfect" gift to someone else? What was it? How did you pick that particular gift for the person? What made it perfect?

_____
_____
_____
_____
_____
_____
_____

Read James 1:17, Romans 6:23, Ephesians 2:8, and Matthew 7:11. God gave us the first and only perfect Christmas gift when Jesus was born. He saw a need we couldn't fill, and He provided the way to satisfy it. It is a gift needed by everyone who has ever lived and ever will live. Take a few moments to reflect on the gift and its Giver. Then, write out a prayer of thanks.

_____
_____
_____
_____
_____
_____
_____

There are many ways people use to ensure their gifts have meaning to those receiving them. Some limit the number, some choose gifts for specific purposes, and others commemorate a special time with a gift that serves as a reminder of that event.

REFLECTING ON CHRISTMAS PAST

How do you give meaning to the gifts you give?

_____
_____
_____
_____
_____
_____
_____
_____

Gifts are not the reason we celebrate Christmas, but like God's gift to us, they can show others they are loved and wanted. Giving is a blessing that blesses both the giver and the receiver. Many won't know the joy of receiving a gift this Christmas due to circumstances beyond their control. How can you bless others who may not otherwise get to share in the joy of giving and receiving this Christmas?

_____
_____
_____
_____
_____
_____
_____
_____

As you reflect on God's gift of Christmas, remember gifts don't have to cost money or come wrapped in pretty paper. Watch for the opportunities God brings you to bless others through giving this Christmas.

THE LOVE

The Love—Day One

1 John 4:19 "We love, because He first loved us."

Awkward Christmas moments. From strange family photos with everyone in matching pajamas to that one side dish at dinner everyone chokes down to avoid offending great-aunt Gertrude—they happen to all of us. Sometimes they make wonderful memories and bring laughter for years to come. Other times, they make you wonder if you've committed the worst holiday *faux pas* possible.

Gift giving tends to fall into this category, at least for me. I am a gift-giver. If I had the funds, I'd give everyone I know a gift at Christmas. I love buying things for others. However, my Christmas budget puts a tight leash on these natural tendencies.

My bank account requires I be selective about purchasing gifts. Some of my friends and loved ones receive gifts from stores. Others receive handmade gifts or a tray of Christmas cookies. But even crafted items aren't free, leaving many without a gift from me at all. It's not feasible.

Do you know what horrifies a gift-giver like me about not being able to buy gifts for everyone? It's the awkward moment when someone gives me a gift, and I don't have one to offer in return. I know they didn't buy me a gift just to receive one, but I do wonder if they're disappointed or if I've accidentally made them feel less special. Am I the only one with this fear?

While this anxiety could stem from a need to not be outdone or to be a people-pleaser, that isn't where my unease over the *faux pas* originates. Thinking a friend might feel they are unimportant to me hurts. The idea they could see themselves as less than a blessing from God saddens me. I want my friends to know I love them.

When it comes to love, God is the ultimate gift-giver. He was and will always be the first to shower us with love. We can't out-love Him.

As early as Genesis, God showed His love for us by gifting us the garden of Eden. Even after we messed that up, God still loved us. He promised a Savior, a way out of the mess we'd created. When Jesus was born, God's love wrapped itself in our fragile flesh and walked among us.

For thirty years, God's love taught us, corrected us, healed us, and offered us hope.

Then, God's love for us was poured out as Jesus was humiliated, beaten, and hung on a cross. It wasn't because of anything He'd done. Jesus offered himself as the sacrifice for our sins.

Even now, God isn't finished showing us His love. He chooses to make us His temple. He chooses to let us participate in spreading the gospel message. God blesses us in countless ways and offers us peace, joy, strength, and forgiveness.

God loved us first and He loves us best.

Without His love, we wouldn't be able to give love back to Him. Because His love overflows in our lives every day, we have love to give back to Him. Everyday. Not just at Christmas.

Daily Reflection: Make a list of the ways God has shown you love, and the ways other people have shown you God's love, especially at Christmas. Place your list in an area where you will see it and you'll remember to meditate on God's love for you. How might you fill this Christmas season with God's love for you and your love for Him?

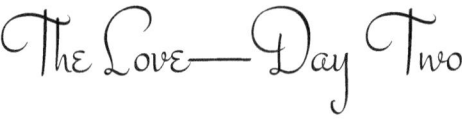

1 Corinthians 13:1-3, 13 "If I speak with the tongues of men and of angels, but do not have love, I have become a noisy gong or a clanging cymbal. If I have the gift of prophecy, and know all mysteries and all knowledge; and if I have all faith, so as to remove mountains, but do not have love, I am nothing. And if I give all my possessions to feed the poor, and if I surrender my body to be burned, but do not have love, it profits me nothing. ... But now faith, hope, love, abide these three; but the greatest of these is love."

It's rare to receive a gift from the office Christmas gift exchange that holds great meaning. The gifts are fun, but something is lost when the present is mandated as a Christmas party activity. Often, the office exchange is carried out white elephant style. Fun or funny gifts, more than useful ones, that aren't purchased with a particular person in mind since they can be traded multiple times.

These gifts may still be memorable. At times, they become tradition as one item shows up year after year. This creates a sense of unity as the group is tied together with this fun memory. But a silly gift passed around year after year doesn't hold the same meaning as the family heirloom passed from oldest daughter to oldest daughter through the generations.

What's often missing in the office gift exchange is love. It's fun and it entertains, providing lighthearted moments to share. But the gift giving isn't done out of love. And love makes all the difference.

As Christmas approaches, social media posts, sweatshirts, and lawn decorations announce the real gift of the season is Jesus. The Son of God coming to become our Savior is the "reason for the season." As cliché as the phrase is, it's also true. But it carries more weight than we acknowledge a lot of times.

Sometimes we toss the truth around from person to person like a white elephant gift at the office Christmas party. We say it. We believe it. But we fail to acknowledge the deep love prompting God's gift.

Our salvation came at the greatest expense. Not only did Jesus leave heaven's throne room, He took on a corruptible body in place of his incorruptible one. Pain, sickness, hunger, and limitations were now part of His day-to-day life. As God, He knew praise and glory were due Him. As a man, Jesus felt every slight and insult.

When the time for His ultimate sacrifice arrived, Jesus heard every taunt. Felt every slap and pull of His beard. Knew the agony of the whips against His skin and the struggle to breathe after being nailed to the cross. He didn't simply experience death. Jesus experienced a horrific death as an innocent man.

Pure, sacrificial love motivated Him. Love for you and me. We are the reason the Creator of the universe lowered Himself to live as His creation. The gift of Jesus's life and death is one given in perfect love. And just like His love, this is the greatest gift we ever receive.

Daily Reflection: Have you experienced God's love at Christmas through the years? Which decorations, music, books, or traditions remind you of God's great gift of love? While personal, God's love and salvation is also meant to be shared. Is there someone in your life who hasn't accepted the greatest, most meaningful Christmas gift of all? How can you share God's amazing love with them this Christmas?

The Love—Day Three

1 John 4:7-11 "Beloved, let us love one another, for love is from God; and everyone who loves is born of God and knows God. The one who does not love does not know God, for God is love. By this the love of God was manifested in us, that God has sent His only begotten Son into the world so that we might live through Him. In this is love, not that we loved God, but that He loved us and sent His Son to be the propitiation for our sins. Beloved, if God so loved us, we also ought to love one another."

I love Christmas movies. When the cheesy Christmas television movies begin, my productivity drops. The movies aren't award winners, but they make you feel good. In some fashion, each one carries the theme of finding joy in giving to others out of love. Compassion in action transforms the confused hero or heroine into the ideal example of what Christmas really means.

While not faith based, these movies point to biblical truth. Christmas is based on love. It's not the feel-good romantic love that puts stars in our eyes and butterflies in our stomachs. It's not the washed-out version of love society teaches where anything goes and feeling good is the goal. It's not even the love that brings together families each Christmas despite differences.

The love of Christmas is real love, God's love. While unconditional, it is often misunderstood. Unconditional doesn't mean anything goes and we're all okay. It means even when we're wrong, the love continues. Unconditional love drove Christ to die for us "while we were yet sinners" and when we "were enemies" with Him. He didn't stop loving us because we were in the wrong. He loved us too much to leave us hopeless.

According to God's example, love is active. We see it in God sending His Son to pay the price for our sin. Our salvation from sin's curse comes from action. But it isn't our action. It's the action of Jesus's death on the cross. It's God doing whatever it takes to redeem us from sin and death.

God's love for us was active then, and it is active now. Even beyond salvation, God's love acts. He doesn't allow us to go down harmful, sinful paths without warning or continue down them without discipline. Sin is never for our good, and God's love won't let Him ignore it in our lives.

God's love isn't only unconditional and active. It's also sacrificial. Christmas gives us warm fuzzies as we think of infant Jesus cradled in Mary's arms while being worshiped by the shepherds. But even in His birth, Jesus's love required sacrifice. The Creator became His creation that night. He gave up His place in heaven being worshiped by angels. He had to contend with loss, sickness, and pain. He knew the disappointment of loved ones doubting Him. He felt the sting of betrayal from close friends. When He hung on the cross, draped in our sins, Jesus knew separation from His Father. His love for us demanded sacrifice.

Daily Reflection: Unconditional, active, and sacrificial. "If God so loved us, we also ought to love one another." What Christmas activities bring God's love to life for you each year? Is there something you can do to encourage taking time to reflect on God's love for you? How can you show that same kind of love to others this Christmas?

The Love—Day Four

Jeremiah 31:3 "The LORD appeared to him from afar, saying, 'I have loved you with an everlasting love; Therefore I have drawn you with lovingkindness.'"

I'm always dreaming of a white Christmas. It's one of the reasons I love living in the Midwest. Growing up, we had snow on Christmas as often as not. Many years, the weather was cold enough we didn't have to wait until December to get our first snow.

Though it doesn't come as early or often now, we still get snow a few times throughout winter. And waking up to a snow-covered landscape on Christmas Day is not unusual.

Sparkling white blankets the brown world. Snow rests on evergreen branches. When sunlight hits the snow, nature provides its own twinkling light show. One might even believe peace has finally come to earth as the hush that accompanies snowfall descends.

Add in a picture window framing a Christmas tree, a fire crackling in the fireplace, and a family opening presents to create a scene worthy of any Americana painting. It's the holiday we all strive to enjoy. A Christmas card come to life.

When a fresh Christmas snow allows the making of homemade snow ice cream, you have a special treat. And of course, you can't forget watching the kids shape a snowman, sledding down a snowy hill, or enjoying a snowball fight. It's worth the piles of coats, gloves, and wet boots discarded when pink-cheeked children come back inside to warm up with a steaming cup of hot cocoa.

Far too soon, the sun returns. The ground warms. Snow gives way to slushy puddles. Muddy tracks appear throughout the house when children—and some adults—forget to remove their shoes. Walking becomes precarious as melting and refreezing snow creates icy patches that are hard to spot.

The beauty of Christmas snow disappears. We hope for its return next year, but we know there is no guarantee of snow at future Christmases.

Christmas snows may be fleeting, but we can always count on God's love. It calls us and invites us to draw close to Him. It's more beautiful that a Christmas snow. Everlasting. Unchanging. Perfect.

From the promises of the coming Savior in the Old Testament to the fulfilling of those prophecies with the birth, life and death of Jesus, God's love for us is overwhelmingly beautiful and wonderfully constant. The best we have to offer cannot make God love us more than He already does. While our sin disappoints, our disobedience never diminishes God's love for us.

Love like this is beyond our imagination. Not even the pristine beauty of a fresh Christmas snow comes close to the perfection of God's love. All it takes to see it is a glance in the manger.

Daily Reflection: God's love is for every day of our lives, but it is so very apparent during the Christmas season. Think back on the ways you've experienced His love during previous Christmases. Take time to praise God for those glimpses into His great love and ask Him to open your eyes to His love this Christmas. Remembering those instances of God's faithful love to you will enable you to add them to your times of celebration and praise during future Christmases.

The Love—Day Five

John 15:9 "Just as the Father has loved Me, I have also loved you; abide in My love."

Everything about the Christmas season is fashioned to foster feelings of family, love, and goodwill. Christmas dinners with the family, cards from loved ones that line our mantles, and Christmas programs at our churches and schools are all meant to draw us closer. Even holiday television commercials use those concepts to encourage you to buy their products.

The dinner rolls and turkeys sold by certain companies are touted as the way to bring a family together around a perfectly set table. If you don't want dessert ruined, you'll buy that specific brand of pumpkin pie, and don't forget the whipped cream made with real whipping cream, not oil. They're really, the commercials want you to believe, the only way to ensure all your holiday guests leave satisfied.

Shopping at one certain department store is the embodiment of what Christmas means, at least, it is if you're to believe the commercial. After all, it is the only store that truly understands the importance of family and the spirit of giving we want to foster at the holidays.

While I don't buy into their hype, either figuratively or literally, I do love a good Christmas-themed commercial. I'm as much a fan of them as I am of a good Christmas movie. They're packed with nostalgia, hope, love, and family. I even have a favorite, though I'm not positive it's aired anymore.

A soldier, the son of the family, arrives back home on Christmas day. His early morning visit is unexpected. Everyone in the house is still asleep. But the son knows how to wake them for their Christmas surprise. He goes into the kitchen, pulls the coffee tin from the shelf, and brews a pot. As the aroma wafts through the house, it beckons to everyone to start the day. Imagine their joy as they come into the kitchen to find not only coffee but their beloved son home for Christmas.

It's family togetherness at its best. Hugs abound and tears flow. Smiles wreathe every face. While it does try to impress on us that coffee is the best way to wake up, the added meaning especially for Christmas is that being together as a family is the best Christmas present.

Family togetherness is powerful. You're not just with each other. You're sharing joys and sorrows. Burdens are lifted more easily. Laughter lightens hearts as everyone reminisces and plays. There is a sharing of each other's lives that deepens your understanding of each other and binds you as one.

This is the kind of relationship God wants to have with us. He sent Jesus to the manger as God with us. After Jesus ascended into heaven, God sent the Holy Spirit to be God in us. He asks us to abide in his love. Soak it up, at Christmas and every day.

Daily Reflection: Abiding in Jesus's love brings joy, strength, encouragement, and a deeper understanding of who He is and who we are in Him. Christmas is the perfect time to sit by the manger and take in God's great love. How can you shape your environment and time this Christmas to encourage abiding in Jesus's love as you celebrate His birth?

Reflecting on the Love

The idea of love is never more prevalent than at Christmas. Everywhere we look, the virtue of loving others is proclaimed. It's important to remember what the world calls love falls short of the love God calls us to. However, Christmas does give us the perfect picture of godly love when we slow down long enough to see it.

How do you define love? Be completely honest, even if it isn't the answer you think you should have.

_____
_____
_____
_____
_____
_____
_____
_____

Does your definition of love match what Scripture tells us love is? How is it similar? Where does it differ?

_____
_____
_____
_____
_____
_____
_____

When you think about the Christmases you've experienced, are there any that serve to remind you of the real definition of love?

_____
_____
_____
_____
_____
_____
_____

When you consider the love God showed us through the first Christmas, what means the most to you?

_____
_____
_____
_____
_____
_____
_____

REFLECTING ON CHRISTMAS PAST

What are some practical ways you can reflect on God's love this Christmas?

_____
_____
_____
_____
_____
_____
_____
_____

In light of God's love for us and His call that we should love others in the same way, what are some practical ways you can show love to others this Christmas?

_____
_____
_____
_____
_____
_____
_____
_____

As you consider God's love, challenge yourself to think beyond the walls of your home. God loved us when we didn't know or love Him. There's a world of people outside our homes and workplaces that we're called to love with the love of God. Ask Him to grow that love in you and show you how to share His love with others.

Your Christmas Heritage

You've completed the devotions for this year's Christmas season. Congratulations! What now?

This devotional is intended for use multiple times over several years. As you go back through the devotions each year, also revisit what God has shown you in previous years. Each page in the *Reflections* section will highlight the themes of the devotions and provide space for you to record special memories. I pray these bring you comfort, joy, and a renewed sense of love each time you reflect on them.

After the journal's pages are full, I encourage you to keep up the tradition of reflection. Use the following pages as a guide in creating a new Christmas journal. You can do this handwritten in a blank journal or with printed pages put in a small binder. The binders, as many as you eventually fill, will be your record of when, where, and how God brought a richness to your Christmas remembrances and celebrations.

Let your journaling remind you of what God has shown you as you revisit your past entries during Christmases to come. One day, you may even want to pass on these records of your Christmas reflections to other loved ones and keep your traditions alive with the next generation.

Annual Reflection Pages

Christmas Reflections 20__

A Time for Remembering

Think back to Christmas last year, but without consulting your journal entry. What do you remember most from that Christmas season?

_____
_____
_____

What would you like to take away from this year's Christmas?

_____
_____
_____

Reflecting on the Reason

What kept you focused on the real reason for Christmas in previous years?

What practical things will you do this year to keep the meaning of Christmas your focus?

REFLECTING ON CHRISTMAS PAST

Reflecting on the Setting

What places and decorations served as the backdrop for your Christmas this year?

_____
_____
_____

Which elements of this Christmas's setting caused you to pause and reflect on Jesus and the holiday's true meaning?

_____
_____
_____

Reflecting on the People

Who played a role in your Christmas celebrations this year? Were they old favorites or newcomers? Who do you wish had been there?

_____
_____
_____

How did you reach beyond yourself to be a blessing to others this Christmas?

_____
_____
_____

Reflecting on the Sounds

Were there any special songs or sounds that spoke to your heart this Christmas?

_____
_____
_____

How did you add your voice of worship to those of the angels and shepherds this Christmas?

_____
_____
_____

Reflecting on the Gifts

Did you give or receive any special gifts this Christmas?

_____
_____
_____

What did God use this Christmas to remind you of His first and perfect Christmas gift, Jesus?

_____
_____
_____

Reflecting on the Love

How did someone show you God's love this Christmas?

_____
_____
_____

How did you show God's love to someone else?

_____
_____
_____

Additional things I'd like to remember

_____
_____
_____

My prayer for the coming year

_____
_____
_____

Christmas Reflections 20__

A Time for Remembering

Think back to Christmas last year, but without consulting your journal entry. What do you remember most from that Christmas season?

_____
_____
_____

What would you like to take away from this year's Christmas?

_____
_____
_____

Reflecting on the Reason

What kept you focused on the real reason for Christmas in previous years?

_____
_____
_____

What practical things will you do this year to keep the meaning of Christmas your focus?

_____
_____
_____

Reflecting on the Setting

What places and decorations served as the backdrop for your Christmas this year?

_____
_____
_____

Which elements of this Christmas's setting caused you to pause and reflect on Jesus and the holiday's true meaning?

_____
_____
_____

Reflecting on the People

Who played a role in your Christmas celebrations this year? Were they old favorites or newcomers? Who do you wish had been there?

_____
_____
_____

How did you reach beyond yourself to be a blessing to others this Christmas?

_____
_____
_____

Reflecting on the Sounds

Were there any special songs or sounds that spoke to your heart this Christmas?

_____
_____
_____

How did you add your voice of worship to those of the angels and shepherds this Christmas?

_____
_____
_____

Reflecting on the Gifts

Did you give or receive any special gifts this Christmas?

_____
_____
_____

What did God use this Christmas to remind you of His first and perfect Christmas gift, Jesus?

_____
_____
_____

Reflecting on the Love

How did someone show you God's love this Christmas?

_____
_____
_____

REFLECTING ON CHRISTMAS PAST

How did you show God's love to someone else?

_____
_____
_____

Additional things I'd like to remember

_____
_____
_____

My prayer for the coming year

_____
_____
_____

Christmas Reflections 20___

A Time for Remembering

Think back to Christmas last year, but without consulting your journal entry. What do you remember most from that Christmas season?

_____
_____
_____

What would you like to take away from this year's Christmas?

_____
_____
_____

Reflecting on the Reason

What kept you focused on the real reason for Christmas in previous years?

_____
_____
_____

What practical things will you do this year to keep the meaning of Christmas your focus?

_____
_____
_____

Reflecting on the Setting

What places and decorations served as the backdrop for your Christmas this year?

_____
_____
_____

Which elements of this Christmas's setting caused you to pause and reflect on Jesus and the holiday's true meaning?

_____
_____
_____

Reflecting on the People

Who played a role in your Christmas celebrations this year? Were they old favorites or newcomers? Who do you wish had been there?

_____
_____
_____

How did you reach beyond yourself to be a blessing to others this Christmas?

_____
_____
_____

Reflecting on the Sounds

Were there any special songs or sounds that spoke to your heart this Christmas?

_____
_____
_____

How did you add your voice of worship to those of the angels and shepherds this Christmas?

_____
_____
_____

Reflecting on the Gifts

Did you give or receive any special gifts this Christmas?

_____
_____
_____

What did God use this Christmas to remind you of His first and perfect Christmas gift, Jesus?

_____
_____
_____

Reflecting on the Love

How did someone show you God's love this Christmas?

_____
_____
_____

REFLECTING ON CHRISTMAS PAST

How did you show God's love to someone else?

_____
_____
_____

Additional things I'd like to remember

_____
_____
_____

My prayer for the coming year

_____
_____
_____

Christmas Reflections 20__

A Time for Remembering

Think back to Christmas last year, but without consulting your journal entry. What do you remember most from that Christmas season?

_____
_____
_____

What would you like to take away from this year's Christmas?

_____
_____
_____

Reflecting on the Reason

What kept you focused on the real reason for Christmas in previous years?

_____
_____
_____

What practical things will you do this year to keep the meaning of Christmas your focus?

_____
_____
_____

REFLECTING ON CHRISTMAS PAST

Reflecting on the Setting

What places and decorations served as the backdrop for your Christmas this year?

_____
_____
_____

Which elements of this Christmas's setting caused you to pause and reflect on Jesus and the holiday's true meaning?

_____
_____
_____

Reflecting on the People

Who played a role in your Christmas celebrations this year? Were they old favorites or newcomers? Who do you wish had been there?

_____
_____
_____

How did you reach beyond yourself to be a blessing to others this Christmas?

_____
_____
_____

Reflecting on the Sounds

Were there any special songs or sounds that spoke to your heart this Christmas?

_____
_____
_____

How did you add your voice of worship to those of the angels and shepherds this Christmas?

_____
_____
_____

Reflecting on the Gifts

Did you give or receive any special gifts this Christmas?

_____
_____
_____

What did God use this Christmas to remind you of His first and perfect Christmas gift, Jesus?

_____
_____
_____

Reflecting on the Love

How did someone show you God's love this Christmas?

_____
_____
_____

REFLECTING ON CHRISTMAS PAST

How did you show God's love to someone else?

_____
_____
_____

Additional things I'd like to remember

_____
_____
_____

My prayer for the coming year

_____
_____
_____

Hosting a Reflecting on Christmas Past Event

While it can be used individually, this devotional is also suitable for use in a women's group. The following pages share how to set up and use the time to minister to the women in your church, small group, or friendship circle. Attendees need their own copies of the devotional journal to use after the event. However, you may make copies of the "Time for Remembering" pages for those who wish to attend the event but cannot purchase their own copy. This will enable their full participation in the day's activities.

PLANNING YOUR EVENT

Set Aside a Time and Place:

The Saturday before advent starts or the first Sunday afternoon or evening of advent is a great time to plan a women's Reflecting on Christmas Past event, provided it doesn't fall on Thanksgiving weekend. This is the beginning of the Christmas season, and the devotions are a great way to focus your celebrations before the season is in full swing. If you can't host your event at the start of advent, take care to avoid other annual holiday happenings in your area. Give yourself at least two and a half hours, more if you want to include a meal or have a group larger than ten.

A home decorated for Christmas will provide a cozy, inviting feel to your event. Keep in mind this will mean extra cleaning time for the host before and after the event. If you want to avoid this during the busy holiday season, the fellowship hall of your church will suffice. But do take time to decorate the room for Christmas. This will help set the mood for the event. If possible, have instrumental Christmas music playing in the background except during the devotional time.

Invitations/Promotion:

Word of mouth is good, but everyone appreciates the added touch of a physical invitation. You can design your own or purchase ready-made holiday invitations. Invite more people than you expect to come because there will be some who cannot make it. Everyone is busy, especially during Christmas, so don't be afraid to make reminder calls to get RSVPs a few days before the event. Also, take advantage of social media by creating an event page on Facebook. When set to private, only those you invite will see information about the event.

If your event is open to all the women of your church, contact someone about getting reminders placed in your church bulletin. Church informational bulletin boards are also a great place to post the invitations.

Refreshments:

Keep it simple. The theme of the event is remembering past Christmases. This means tradition plays a large part in what you're doing. Ask everyone to bring their favorite family Christmas cookie/candy and the recipe to share. Have them bring multiple copies of the recipe so everyone leaves with a copy of each dish brought.

Spiced cider, hot cocoa, coffee, and hot tea are great drink choices for a Christmas event. Cider and cocoa can be made ahead of time and kept warm in a crock-pot. Holiday mugs are a fun choice for serving, but if you prefer to avoid extra clean up, disposable cups may be the way to go.

REFLECTING ON CHRISTMAS PAST

The Schedule:

- **Welcome everyone, thank those who helped plan the event, and open with prayer** (10 minutes)
- **A Time for Remembering:** In the spirit of remembering Christmases past, everyone was asked to bring a favorite family Christmas treat to share. Let the women fill their plates and mingle for a few minutes. This will give stragglers time to arrive. You do not have to wait until everyone is done before going to the next part, but give a five-minute warning to get refills or use the restroom before you start. (15-20 minutes depending on the size of your group)
- **The Reason:** Read through the "Time for Remembering" devotion that starts the book. When you reach the reflection part, pass out books and a pen. If people did not order books, pass out stapled copies of the first devotion. Allow a few minutes to fill in the answers. Provide time for people to share their answers, but don't push. (30 minutes)
- **The Sound:** End your devotional time with one or two traditional Christmas carols. (10 minutes)
- **The Setting:** Our environment makes a difference in our mood and focus. Discuss favorite decorations and have a list of decorating tricks and tips to present. Pinterest is a great place for ideas. You may want to add a simple craft project to this time. If you make a holiday decoration, consider an old-fashioned one in keeping with the Christmas past theme. (20-30 minutes)
- **The People:** Reach out as a group to others in need. Make simple Christmas cards to send to veterans, overseas military, those in nursing homes, or your church's shut-ins. Or prepare cards for emergency workers and arrange for the group to deliver them on Christmas Eve or Christmas Day. (20 minutes)
- **The Gifts:** Ask participants to share a memorable gift they've received. Discuss various gift giving options that are either inexpensive or free. Choose a simple gift for everyone to make. Some ideas include shaped soaps, candy filled jars with a

personalized gift tag, hot cocoa mix, a mini manicure set, or a candle holder. Again, Pinterest is a great place to find ideas. (20 minutes)
- **The Love**: Encourage everyone to choose one person to love through the season anonymously. Commit to praying for that person every day. Perform random acts of kindness for them throughout the Christmas season. (5 minutes)
- **Wrapping It Up:** Thank everyone for coming. Make sure they take home their collection of recipes. Remind them to read and fill out their devotional books for the rest of the week, using them to set the tone for the rest of the season. End with prayer.

About the Author

Heather Greer loves all things Christmas. Though her family groans every time, Heather has been known to play Christmas music year-round. They run from the room in horror every July when Heather begins watching Christmas movies. But Heather doesn't care. Who doesn't want a little Christmas spirit by mid-year?

Though her help decorating the Christmas tree each year has dwindled, none of her family says no to the dozens of Christmas cookies she bakes each December. Heather doesn't hold it against them though. Christmas treats are the best sweets.

While fun, Heather's Christmas traditions are not her main focus each December. God's love and the hope He offers are seen clearly through the yearly celebration of Jesus's birth. It's these things, the real reasons for joy and peace, that Heather wants to focus on each Christmas. These truths are what Heather weaves into each story and devotion she writes. And she prays for God to use everything she writes in the lives of readers, drawing them closer to Him.

Also by Heather Greer

***Window of Opportunity* by Heather Greer**

The Stained-glass Legacy Series—Book One

Faith and duty drive Evangeline Moore to protect her father's pristine image as a judge in Harrisburg, Illinois. Her resolve's biggest test? Dot, her childhood friend. With Evangeline beside her, Dot's desire for the Roaring Twenties' glitz and glamor leads the pair into questionable situations.

Born into a Chicago mob family, Brendan Dunne understands duty, but faith puts him at odds with his father's demands. Even when his brother James's propensity for trouble lands them in Harrisburg, the truth is undeniable. To their father, the lines he won't cross mean Brendan will never measure up.

When circumstances push Brendan and Evangeline together, unexpected events create opportunity to break free of family expectations. Will they be brave enough to forge their own path before the window closes on their chance to change?

Get your copy here:

https://scrivenings.link/windowofopportunity

Love in the Squared Circle

by **Heather Greer**

Trinity Knight is not a fan of professional wrestling. But with her husband gone, it falls to her to give their son the father-son trip they daydreamed about when he was alive. After Trinity causes them to miss a meet and greet with Jay's favorite wrestler, a random act of kindness saves the trip and starts Trinity on an unexpected path.

Universal Wrestling Organization Champion Blane Sterling hears whiny children at photo ops all the time. However, overhearing a young boy comfort his mother piques his interest. Touched by their story, Blane works with the UWO Public Relations team to give Jay the experience of a lifetime.

As they learn each other's stories, Trinity and Blane are drawn to each other. But they don't just come from different states. They live in different worlds. Trinity might learn to fit into his life, but can those in her world look beyond Blane's profession to see his heart? Or will a lack of acceptance cause Trinity and Blane to lose their shot at love?

Get your copy here:

https://scrivenings.link/loveinthesquaredcircle

Cake That!

Third-place Winner - Contemporary Romance
2022 Selah Awards
Ten bakers. Nine days. One winner.

Competing on the *Cake That* baking show is a dream come true for Livvy Miller, but debt on her cupcake truck and an expensive repair make her question if it's one she should chase. Her best friend, Tabitha, encourages Livvy to trust God to care for The Sugar Cube, win or lose.

Family is everything to Evan Jones. His parents always gave up their dreams so their children could achieve theirs. Winning *Cake That* would let him give back some of what they've sacrificed by allowing him to give them the trip they've always talked about but could never afford.

As the contestants live and bake together, more than the competition heats up. Livvy and Evan have a spark from the start, but they're in it to win. Neither needs the distraction of romance. Unwanted attention from Will, another competitor, complicates matters. Stir in strange occurrences to the daily baking assignments, and everyone wonders if a saboteur is in the mix.

With the distractions inside and outside the *Cake That* kitchen, will Livvy or Evan rise above the rest and claim the prize? Or does God have more in store for them than they first imagined?

Get your copy here:
scrivenings.link/cakethat

Love Delivered

A novella collection—including "Sweet Delivery"

by Heather Greer

Sweet Delivery (by Heather Greer)—After winning Cake That, Will Forrester thinks his Pastry Perfect Baking Dreams have come true. The sweetness fades when a chain bakery moves to town, and Will must adjust his plans to keep his customers. Hiring Erica Gerard is one of those changes. As they work together, Erica challenges Will and offers new ideas to improve the bakery. Soon, Erica and Will start bringing out the best in each other. But Erica harbors a secret, and if it's discovered, Will might never be the same.

Get your copy here:

https://scrivenings.link/lovedelivered

Faith, Hope, and Love Series:

Faith's Journey

Faith, Hope, and Love Series - Book One

https://scrivenings.link/faithsjourney

Grasping Hope

Faith, Hope, and Love Series - Book Two

https://scrivenings.link/graspinghope

Relentless Love

Faith, Hope, and Love Series - Book Three

https://scrivenings.link/relentlesslove

www.ingramcontent.com/pod-product-compliance
Lightning Source LLC
Chambersburg PA
CBHW052143070526
44585CB00017B/1948